THE

ATLANTIC

OCEAN ROWING RACE

2007

THE

ATLANTIC

OCEAN ROWING RACE
2007

Steve Gardner

First published in the United Kingdom in 2013 by
The Cloister House Press

ISBN 978-1-909465-00-8

The Reason Why

"THE BOOK OF THE BLOG"

A Real, honest to goodness True Life Adventure, of how one ordinary Pink Plastic Pig, one ordinary nocturnal Mid Atlantic Black Bag Gorilla and two ordinary blokes with oars, attempted to row in the "World's Toughest Rowing Race", a three thousand mile race across The Atlantic Ocean, in "The Reason Why" under the watchful eye of "The Grinning Turk" ....and became extraordinary.

Come with us on a fantastic voyage of adventure across one of the World's most hostile environments, writing poetry and meeting "friends" along the way. The race organisers, Woodvale Challenge, state in their literature that the number of people to successfully row across an Ocean, is less than the number of people who have been in space, or who have climbed Mount Everest, so how can you turn down the chance to join us, in what was and still is a life changing experience.

"You'll be glued to it…like I was" – Droops the Watch Pig

"It's full of rubbish…like I was" – Gus the nocturnal Mid Atlantic Black Bag Gorilla

"A tale as free as a sea breeze…like I was…till I crashed into them"–Pete the Petrel

(additional notes and memories, or "Porkscripts", by Droops The Watch Pig)

For my wife and our children, Samantha, Rebecca and Oliver, with love.

Somewhere over the horizon

Lie the shores of paradise

English Harbour sits there waiting

With the rum punch and the ice

What a welcome will await you

Smell the land upon the breeze

No more junk and salty water

For you hero's of the seas

Let no fickle wind deter you

Laugh out loud at ocean swell

One last pull now to the finish

And what a tale you'll have to tell

sg2008

CONTENTS

Page 5   Opening Poem – Somewhere Over The Horizon

Page 9   Random Memory No. 1

Page 11   Song Of The Western Men

Page 13   Meet The Rowers

Page 17   Porkscript No. 1

Page 19   Chapter 1 – In the Beginning

Page 25   Chapter 2 – Dot Watching

Page 28   Porkscript No. 2

Page 29   Life Before Mo

Page 33   Random Memory No. 2

Page 37   The Atlantic Rowing Race 2007

Page 39   Chapter 3 - The How, When, What, Where but no mention of Why…

Page 46   Porkscript No. 3

Page 47   Random Memory No. 3

Page 49   Chapter 4 - The "Pre-Race Blog"

Page 69   Random Memory No. 4

Page 70   Porkscript No. 4

Page 71   Chapter 5 – La Gomera…the End of the Beginning

Page 90   Strange But True

Page 91   Random Memory No. 5

Page 93   Chapter 6 – Finally The Start and the "Race Blog"

Page 143   (Not so) Random Memory No. 6

Page 149   Porkscript No.5 – "The Arrival"

Page 170   Official Race Placings, Results, Daily Mileage and Position Records

Page 180   Chapter 7 – Antigua

Page 185   Random Memory No. 7

Page 191   Chapter 8 – "The Post Race Blog"

Page 199   Thank You – Sponsor list

Page 201   The Sam Quote of the Day – Answers

Page 202   Acknowledgements

Page 204   Epilogue – So What Happens Now

Page 205   Closing Poem – The Moonlight Trail

Random Memory No.1 – 1ST January 2008... Mid Atlantic

I stood up and unbuckled my safety harness, tripping over the elasticated leash attached to the boat lifeline for the forty second time, and watched with a slightly manic and sadistic pleasure as the elastic sprang back violently, clattering the stainless clasp heavily into the bulkhead.

This was after scrambling forward from the bow rowing position, in the dark, hitting the mid ships rowing position, bouncing off the gunnel of the boat and stumbling headlong into the foot well like a fairy elephant and slamming into the aft cabin hatch with a resounding thud! I thanked "Mo" for her precise timing in choosing the exact moment to throw a particularly large and unfriendly wave at us, but She was especially good at that.

As I was performing this personal Olympic obstacle race over two metres of the most impossibly cluttered, and perpetually moving deck, Paul was doing the same the other side...only in reverse, for this was rowing changeover, and we did this fairly basic but decidedly hazardous manoeuvre, literally 20 times every day !

Paul clambered into the rowing seat...then stood up again, his backside hovering over it as he rearranged foam and sheepskin padding, and adjusted the coils of rope beneath it, that formed our unlikely, but surprisingly effective cradle, devised to keep the most damaged and painful parts of our ever deteriorating backsides, suspended, away from the sores and pressure points.

Harness off, I tucked it under the gunnel, and continued to struggle with the lurching boat, as I tried to unpop, unzip and unclip my big red coat, which originally, I had never thought we would need to wear, but the nights could be sometimes cold, and were always wet, so it had become an essential. Eventually I succeeded, opened the hatch, threw in the coat and turned just in time to see a big fizzer of a wave appear out of the blackness and hit the side of the boat, sending spray all over the now gingerly sitting Paul. He looked up at me as I was about to disappear into the warm, dry, relative calm of the aft cabin, and there was water dripping from his hood, beard and nose, and just for a fleeting moment I had the irrational thought that my life was in danger....but Paul merely leant forward and unscrewed a deck hatch and took out his forty second energy "Go" bar of the day, then leaned back against the forward cabin to eat it, as if in defiance. Rowing had been temporarily suspended, and I appeared safe... at least for the time being!

I opened the hatch once more and entered backwards as I usually did, "See you in a couple of hours" I called, but saw his i-pod earphones in place, so he didn't hear me. He was off in his audio book fighting Fluffy the three headed dog with Harry Potter.

I closed the hatch and struggled to turn in the tight space of the cabin, from my kneeling position, to flop down head to stern. As usual I banged my head on the cabin roof, and was thrown sideways by another well timed wave, just as I was off balance, right into the radar and electrics panel. This time I merely head butted the AIS radar and turned on the VHF radio, on previous occasions I had hit the power button, turned everything off and plunged us into complete darkness...and could I find the damn thing to turn it back on again?

I lay there damp and sticky, rubbing my head, and took off my wet shorts and top, and felt better laying naked on my towel, although this too was damp and caked with salt.

I turned to face "my wall" and the photos of my wife and children, and straight away felt the now familiar lump of emotion appear in my throat...I longed to see them all...I even missed old "Baggins" our dog. I quickly dismissed any thought of a tear. Only one way to get back to them, and that means rowing to Antigua...there is no other way from here, a thousand miles from anywhere, crying won't help, that's for sure. We chose to do this, and in the relative calm of the "Blue Marlin" bar, holding on to a pint of beer for support, we had made a pact that we WILL enjoy it!

What the hell am I doing here, crossed my mind once again, and not for the last time.....

.....five seconds later, or at least that's what it felt like, the hatch opened, and there was Paul, "Oi...your turn...that's two hours!"

"Sorry, forgot the alarm again" I groaned

("Mo" – Taken from my poem to The Atlantic "Mighty Ocean")

Incidentally, this is a two way memory, and works exactly the same in reverse, (except for the family and dog, of course), when I was rowing and Paul was resting, especially the "forgot the alarm" bit, you can just change the names round!

Song Of The Western Men

This song was written in 1825 by Robert Stephen Hawker (3rd Dec 1803-15th Aug 1875), the vicar of Morewenstowe, and is sung as the unofficial Anthem of Cornwall, and often referred to, as simply "Trelawny"

The Trelawny to which the song relates, was one "Jonathon Trelawny"(1650-1721), who was one of the seven Bishops imprisoned in The Tower of London, by James ll in 1688 for opposing The King's permissive legislation towards Roman Catholics.

The Bishops went on trial for libel, but were acquitted... a victory for Cornwall.

A good sword and a trusty hand, a merry heart and true!

King James' men shall understand what Cornish lads can do!

And have they fixed the where and when, and shall Trelawny die?

Here's twenty thousand Cornishmen will know The Reason Why!

And shall Trelawny live?

And shall Trelawny die?

Here's twenty thousand Cornishmen

Will know The Reason Why!

Out spake their Captain brave and bold, a merry wight was he:

If London Tower were Michael's hold, we'd set Trelawny free!

We'll cross The Tamar, land to land, The Severn is no stay:

With "one and all," and hand in hand, and who shall bid us nay?

And shall Trelawny Live?

And shall Trelawny die?

Here's twenty thousand Cornishmen

Will know The Reason Why!

And when we come to London Wall, a pleasant sight to view,

Come forth! Come forth! ye cowards all, here's men as good as you   .

Trelawny he's in keep and hold, Trelawny he may die:

But here's twenty thousand Cornish bold, will know The Reason Why!

And shall Trelawny live?

And shall Trelawny die?

Here's twenty thousand Cornishmen

Will know The Reason Why!

Yours Truly Steve Gardner and Paul Harris enjoy a little après row

in Muiden, near Amsterdam, at the annual Muiden-Pampus-Muiden regatta,

in November 2006, one year before the start of The Atlantic Rowing race.

By the time of the start of The Atlantic Rowing Race 2007, I would be 51 years old and Paul would be 46. We are both married, Paul and his wife Dawn have two children, Jake and Danielle, my wife Christine and I have three children, Samantha, Rebecca and Oliver.

I work as a Contracts Manager in the construction industry for Wombwell Homes, in Lostwithiel, while Paul works as a technician for Western Power Distribution in Pool.

We are both members of Zennor Gig Club, based in Penzance, Cornwall, and have been friends, rowing together continuously, for the past ten years. As part of the mens A crews, mixed crews and veteran crews at regattas every weekend of the Summer, at the end of season at Newquay County Championships, and of course the annual World Championships on The Isles of Scilly each May. Then there are the away days!

In 2002, we were two of the seventeen Zennor club members to row over 200 miles down The River Danube, through Germany and Austria, finishing up in Vienna a week later. We were treated to several days of wonderful hospitality, staying at Passau Rowing Club, in Germany, and taking part in their "Kneipen" rowing regatta. Then it was time to go, and we launched the Gig in Passau on The Danube, and rowed to a different campsite along the river each night. This meant that tents had to be dismantled and erected, before and after a full day's rowing. The logistics of this trip were immense, and would never have been possible without the unfailing support and generous assistance of Passauer Ruderverein (Passau Rowing Club), and of course my friend, the amazing and irrepressible Claus Hein, who put all the German side together, and somehow managed to make it work, even for seventeen "totally disorganized bloody English!" as he so eloquently put it!

In 2005, The Club travelled to Venice to take part in the traditional rowing spectacular, "The Vogalonga", around the lagoon, Venetian islands and canals of this fantastic city, the first Cornish pilot gig to do so. And after the celebrations, we set off with Passau Rowing Club (and Claus of course !), once more, back to Germany, and The Danube. This time for a 180 km. row from upstream of Passau, ending in Deggendorf, from where we drove on to Passau for the weekend. (this does leave a 50 km. gap in The Danube that remains as yet un rowed…maybe one day…).

In 2006, we, again as part of Zennor Gig Club, (at the time we called it the "ZIG" Club…Zennor International Gig Club, but this later became "GROT"…Gig Rowers On Tour), travelled to Muiden, Holland, near Amsterdam, for the Muiden-Pampus-Muiden annual regatta…and boy do those Dutch know how to party !!

Paul and myself feeling a little too comfortable in Amsterdam…

… and sharing a drink with Charlestown all in our Dutch caps, Holland, November 2006.

Above, Paul and myself approaching The Rialto Bridge Venice for "The Vogalonga" 2005
And below, Sennen Cove to Isles of Scilly, 28 miles - 6 hours 11 mins, Aug. 2006

The sun beats down relentlessly, burning my skin, and the salt wind, varying between light breeze and violent squall, blows without pause, depositing layers of salt all over my naked, pink body.

Occasionally, great waves break over the cabin and it is all I can do to stay on board, while at other times, they hit the side of the boat, sending a wall of spray over everything... including me !

I was being bleached, and with every day that went on, I was fading. I was also having trouble with my voice, once loud, clear and strong, now only a whisper of its' former self.

My nose was burnt, irreversibly...my legs and feet ached from being stuck in the same place for so long, with nowhere to walk, run or even stretch properly. The necklace I had been given, and was stupid enough to wear, seemed to be made from "binder twine," and it was making my neck sore.

Any minute now, that bloke...the big bald headed one...is going to fling open the cabin hatch just below me, and spring out with annoying cheerfulness, and proclaim to virtually nobody at all, (but that won't stop him !), that it is " A New Dawn !"

Then he will turn his attention to me, and squeeze my middle till I let out what is now a pathetic little croak of an oink, and he'll say, "Morning Droops"... I'll give him a new dawn... one of these days I'm going to oink him in the eye!!

This is the story of "DROOPS", The Watch Pig, and his remarkable and epic voyage across 3000 miles of The Mighty Atlantic Ocean, aided slightly, but mostly hindered by two blokes with oars, who seemed to be labouring under the misconception, that they were in charge!

MEET DROOPS…THE WATCH PIG

Torn from his life as a plaything
To cross The Atlantic for fun
The horizon he scanned
For some mud, grass or sand
By the light of the moon and the sun.

From morning till night he kept watching
Only wave after wave did he spy
With nowhere to snuffle
For root, bulb or truffle
He would oink, with his snout, at the sky.

Chapter 1.   In The Beginning

'Twas a wild and stormy Cornish night, and although this was 1994, to anyone peering around the door of The Tinners Arms, it could have been 1694!

The few locals that had ventured out, were huddled around the open fire, and in the dim flickering light, could easily have been mistaken for smugglers or wreckers, talking over evil deeds and secret plans.

In Zennor, time stands still…from the giants lurking in the granite quoits high above, to the Knockers far below in the mines, Piskey in the fields, and The Mermaid down in the crashing waves of the cove…there is still the possibility of magic.

After four pints of H.S.D. (Hicks Special Draught, known locally as High Speed Death!), there is even more possibility of magic. So when one wise fool (who shall remain nameless), said, "Why don't we start our own gig club?"… "Why don't we get our own gig?"… "Why don't we blast out a section of cliff from The North Cornish Coast, construct a passable road to the cove, and clear the beach of 500,000 tonnes of granite boulders?… and "Why don't we have another pint ?"…you can understand the strength of resolve here, if I tell you that three out of these four original objectives were quickly accomplished…especially the "another pint" one, (you can probably guess which of the four is still quite some way off !!).

So this was my introduction to rowing, and since that fateful night in The Tinners Arms, Zennor, thirteen years had passed, during which time, I have been part of a crew for Zennor Gig Club that was to come 5th in the World Championships at Scilly; rowed 200 miles and 180 miles on The River Danube, in two separate trips; have taken part in "The Vogalonga" in Venice, and Muiden-Pampus-Muiden, in Amsterdam, all of which have already been mentioned. In addition, we became County Mixed Veteran Champions in 2006; have rowed the relatively short, but treacherous stretch of The Atlantic between Sennen Cove (Lands End) and The Isles of Scilly, and have competed in several London River Races, on The Thames, between Richmond and The Isle of Dogs (22miles).

Now, the most improbable event of all, is finding myself on an overnight train, (without a berth!), leaving Penzance Station on a cold and wet November night, wearing a sweatshirt, jeans and flip-flops, with no luggage except a wallet, a passport and one way tickets to Gatwick by train and Tenerife by plane. Once in Tenerife, I was to get a taxi to a ferry port I had never been to, and buy a one way ferry ticket to a small Canary Island I had never heard of, where I was to be hopefully reunited with a 23 foot long plywood rowing boat, I had helped to build over the previous Winter, and then proceed to row it in a race, 3000 miles across The Atlantic Ocean to Antigua!

Looking back now at all of this, there is a very obvious link between them all, as in all of these crews, rowing alongside me, was one Paul Harris.

Now guess who is sitting opposite me on that night train from Penzance, wearing only a sweatshirt, no luggage except passport and similar tickets, (he was actually carrying a plastic bag full of Pringles and out of date Budweiser, but we soon got rid of those!).

Paul Harris has a long rowing pedigree, (unlike me), man and boy, stretching back into the mists of time. We won a trophy once that had his name on it, "Presented to Paul Harris" for winning a pair of paddles race in the 1970's or 80's, and the trophy was being reused for a gig race.

"What the hell am I doing here ?" …I thought… not for the last time…as the train hurtled on through the black, cold, wet, November night…

Chris my wife, Me, Kathy Hawkins, Jennie Richards, Roger Warren, Paul Harris and John Lindfield, the "Vogalonga crew", Venice, May 2005. Claus Hein is in the green below.

After Venice, we drove through the Alps to Germany, and the River Danube …

This is Passau, the river Ilz joins The Danube here … and the river Inn joins in too!

We launched at a little place called Staubing, after being treated to a feast the night before, and rowed to Weltonburg Abbey, Kelheim, Regensburg, Straubing and Deggendorf, over the next five days. We were supposed to row back to Passau to complete the link, as we rowed 200 miles from Passau to Vienna in 2002, but we ran out of time and had to get the gig out at Deggendorf, so there is a 50 kilometre or so gap to fill in some day…

Passau, from the magnificent cathedral, the palace on the hill, the rowing club, the way the mighty Danube flows through picking up the river Ilz and the river Inn, the town, the Weissbeer, the Irish Bar! All I can say is if you get a chance to go … then go, it's brilliant!

THE DAY THE TRAINING PAID OFF
JULY 1ST 2006
SALTASH

ZENNOR MIXED VETERAN CREW
WIN THEIR CLASS AND BECOME
COUNTY CHAMPIONS

Steve Gardner James Morris-Marsham (Coxswain) Guy Lichfield Paul Harris
Vanessa Bush Jennie Richards Fiona Hewett

The 5th place men's crew Isles of Scilly World Championships 2006

Waiting for the start, Ham House, Richmond, London River Race September 11th 2004, Jen took the photo, and below, looking down to Kingston-upon-Thames and the start line.

Front to back- Jennie Richards, Kathy Hawkins, Bob Robinson, Me, Richard Cornish, James Morris Marsham, Matt Hopson. Paul is coxing, and taking the photographs.

The Great London River Race, September 11th 2004

Paul gets the port … I get to throw away my socks and trainers …

….and that's why!! Jennie took these shots.

Chapter 2 – Dot Watching

August Bank Holiday Monday 2005, Newlyn Fish Festival… the annual gathering of local crafts and food stalls, exhibitions and demonstrations, celebrating all things fishy in the confines of Newlyn fishing harbour… the smells are, well… amazing !

As usual it was complete mayhem, with wall to wall people squeezing around the narrow spaces between stalls, straining to see cooking demonstrations and the life boat display, buying raffle tickets and watching the gig race of course, eating burgers and pasties, scallops and mussels, ice cream and candy floss.

There are always, any number of historic and working fishing boats on display, but this year saw a different kind of boat as well. A hand built, hand painted, ungainly looking top heavy plywood rowing boat, apparently of a special design, to enable two nut cases to row across The Atlantic Ocean!

Paul had told me that his long time rowing buddy, Chris Barrett, and his mate Bob Warren, were in the advanced stages of fundraising and boat preparation, having entered themselves in the 2005 Woodvale Atlantic Rowing Race.

About the only thing I found attractive about this idea, was that it was to finish in Antigua, but the thought of actually taking part in a race such as this, had not yet appeared in the remotest corner of my imagination, and gave me "the willies" just thinking about it.

"Bloody flimsy little boat like that, being bounced all over The Atlantic, for how long 50, 60 days, you must be joking, or out of your mind. You wouldn't catch me out there in that!" I had been heard to say on several occasions. But here we were, looking at Chris and Bob's pride and joy, "The Spirit of Cornwall", and now I was standing directly in front of it, in the flesh, so to speak, it made not a bit of difference. Of course I told Chris how good She looked, but the thought splashing about in forty foot waves in my head, was still, "you wouldn't catch me out there in that!"

The final nail in the proverbial coffin was the cost…"HOW MUCH?" I exclaimed loudly, as Paul calmly announced that the cost altogether for a pairs boat to be bought and built, fitted out with all the necessary equiptment and entry fees for the race etc, was in the order of £65,000 ! (this was the Woodvale estimate if you got them to do most of it for you). I think the word stupid joined the word mad, and they both surfed the same forty foot wave in my head, but this time disappeared over the horizon. However, just like a spilled bag of chicken feed, an unnoticed and as yet un-germinated seed, lay there as good as planted.

August turned into September, September into October, and October into November, and I can't say that I had given a lot of thought to The Atlantic Rowing Race, The Spirit of Cornwall, or Chris and Bob, until one day when Paul said they had gone, and the race was due to start on November 30th !

Although later on, we were both driven mad by constantly being asked the same questions over and over again, at this stage I was guilty of doing the same…….

"Where does it go from?"

"La Gomera" said Paul

"Never heard of it"

"One of The Canary Islands, off Tenerife" said Paul

"And it finishes in Antigua"

"Yes" said Paul

"How far is it?"

"About 3000 miles" said Paul

"Wow, makes our 200 miles down The Danube look a bit tame, don't you think?"

"Um…" said Paul, deep in thought

"Still don't fancy that much…Antigua sounds alright, it's the getting there! How long will it take?"

"Fifty to sixty days or so" said Paul

"Blimey!"

The 2005 race day arrived, but bad weather delayed the start, and November moved uneasily and choppily into December, and whilst they were stuck in the harbour, waiting for the weather to allow them to start, an inshore race was thought up to keep them busy, and the La Gomera Cup was born.

One day, a week or so before Christmas, Paul started talking about Chris and Bob's progress, the race having finally started, and about the Woodvale website where you could watch their, and all the others too, little coloured dots, inch their way, ever so slowly across the enormous expanse of blue, that was The Atlantic Ocean.

So I looked it up, became conversant with all the boats in the race, their websites, blogs, photos and of course their ever changing positions as shown by their little coloured dots. It was addictive, and pretty soon I was hooked. Switching on the computer to check on progress and reading daily blogs, and watching those dots, became the first job of the day…….every day……several times a day, and it effectively took over my life both at work and at home.

I just couldn't believe all these little coloured dots were boats, and in each one of them were people, rowing. Rowing when I got up, rowing when I went to bed, rowing while I was at work, rowing while I ate dinner…breakfast…supper…and it stunned me to think, that if I got up for a pee in the night, they were still out there, way out there in the dark, still bloody rowing! Christmas Day, Boxing Day, rowing, New Years Eve, New Years Day, rowing… always rowing. How must they be feeling, how did they cope so far from life and land, out on the ocean… in the middle of the ocean a thousand miles from anything, at Christmas too.

I yearned for more information, who were these people? I sat waiting by the computer for updated blogs and message boards. The weather did not seem good, several boats had been capsized, and we later learned that the so called "window" in the hurricane season, (November to March, which is why the race goes at this time), was not much more than a slit this year, and they were experiencing the worst weather in this area at this time of year for 200 years!

January 2006 wore on, and my regular daily routine was well established, when disaster struck. I was listening to the radio, through earphones, on the train to work one morning, when the words, "two Cornish rowers had to be rescued yesterday, after suffering a capsize in very rough seas, 180 miles off Antigua…"

I couldn't believe what I was hearing, apparently a freak wave had pitch poled them (stern over bow capsize), and for whatever reason, the self righting boat didn't self right! They tried, but to no avail, and had to set off their E.P.I.R.B. (Emergency Position Indicating Radio Beacon), a mandatory piece of safety equipment for all boats in the race, and take to the life raft.

Amazingly, it was Falmouth Coastguard who picked up the distress beacon, all those thousands of miles away, and coordinated the rescue.

I exclaimed out loud on the train, I couldn't believe it, not them…not now, so close, having rowed all that way, over 2750 miles, only to fall short by 180 miles or so. It was more than I could bear, let alone Chris and Bob! How must they be feeling? At least they were safe, but they must be devastated, I know I would be.

In the days that followed, photographs appeared on websites of Chris and Bob with their families all together in Antigua, and as other boats and rowers arrived, one by one the little coloured dots closed in on the bottom corner of the big green blob of Antigua.

All in all, 6 boats never made it to Antigua, but thankfully all the rowers were rescued and were safe.

Suddenly, however, there were no new blogs, no new photos, and worst of all, no dots to watch! What the hell was I going to do now, I had become addicted to watching the dots, and my days were now empty of the excitement of it all. It was almost as if I had been a part of the race itself, it had become so real and important to me…and now it was gone!

Post Script: "The Spirit of Cornwall", Chris and Bob's capsized boat, rubbed salt in the wound somewhat, by making its' own way, courtesy of wind and waves, to within 5 km of Antigua, a couple of weeks later, and was pulled ashore by local fishermen.

Post Script 2: It is worth noting that in the 2005 race, the New Zealand boat " Team Sun Latte", and the American boat, " American Fire", both suffered the indignity of a capsize, with both crews having to be subjected to dramatic rescues. It is therefore remarkable, that Tara Remington from "Team Sun Latte", Emily Kohl and Sarah Kessans from "American Fire", together with Jo Davies, who had to be airlifted from "Rowgirls", after suffering a back injury, have joined forces as a rowing four, to have another go in the 2007 renewal.

In their boat "Unfinished Business", which speaks for itself, they have put behind them their bad experiences of the 46th day of the 2005 race, and it shows great courage and resolve to go out there and try again…and they all have our utmost respect.

In all there were 6 capsizes, with subsequent retirements from the 2005 race, and of the ones not mentioned here, the story of "Moveahead", has to be the strangest, but I will talk a bit more about that later.

How had I got here? The first I knew about anything was being woken up and dragged off to a pub, apparently to watch 8 women throw metal pointy things at a target on a wall! They did this non-stop, for 24 hours*, and it must have been hard and thirsty work judging by the amount they ate and drank! Sometimes in the depths of despair, sometimes accompanied by hysterical singing…if you can call it that… and after every throw, I was squeezed and made to oink!

Eventually they left me alone, for increasingly long periods, only for some bloke to turn up at the 11th hour (or possibly it was the 23rd hour), grabbed me from where I was quietly sitting minding my own business, and proceeded to squeeze me and make me oink after every throw again. Everyone seemed to think it immensely funny…ha bloody ha!

Then, before I knew what was happening, I had been named "Droops", I even had it written in felt tip on my belly, and had been presented as a mascot, whatever that is, and was to go off with this bloke and his mate, across The Atlantic…whatever that was…well, I know now !

But then what happened to mascot? Having found out what a mascot did…not a lot, I was looking forward to quietly sitting out of the way in the cabin, only to have my job description changed to "Watch Pig!"

Then, the other bloke…the quiet one…went and super glued my feet to the top of the cabin roof…they say watch out for the quiet ones!

So here I am, literally stuck to the cabin roof, totally exposed to wind, rain, sun and that big beastly blue expanse of nothing all around us, known respectfully as The Atlantic Ocean, but who these two drongo's seem to have christened "Mo".

Whatever it's called, it constantly tries to throw me overboard and keep me wet. At least they have attached me to a necklace, as a life line, fixed to the boat, even if it is only a tatty old bit of "bailer twine!"

"Woke up this Morning!"**..Oh yes, the music, same track every morning, give us a break!"…got a blue moon in your eye…" it says, I'll give them a blue moon in their eye if they don't play something different!

* 24 hour darts marathon fundraiser, thanks to Karen at Wombwell Homes for organizing it, and the splendid Globe Inn, Lostwithiel, for letting her stage it there, October 2007.

** "Woke Up This Morning"- by The Alabama 3 (Theme to "The Sopranos"), became a daily ritual every morning.

LIFE BEFORE MO

Across the very Ocean wide
On wooden steeds we try to ride
Beneath the sun, above the moon
We must be off to Scilly soon

Where all those steeds of every hue
The good ones green, the bad ones blue *
Will dance across the endless sea
And we will be there, you and me

Between St. Agnes and the quay
We'll ride the waves of destiny
Upon a Mermaid fast and fair
Both you and me, this dream we share

Then when the steeds are safe ashore
The Ocean Gods alone to roar
That light of hope shines from afar
For you and me in The Mermaid bar.

* Private joke with our friends from Devoran Gig Club, our gigs are green, guess what colour theirs are…

The Mermaid, St.Mary's, and "Bruno", the only dog I know to get an asbo! Sadly deceased.

29

It was The Isles of Scilly World Gig Championships 2006, and I spent two hours on The Scillonian, on the way from Penzance, talking to Chris Barrett about his Atlantic row, and the capsize of "The Spirit of Cornwall" just four months previous. But at this time, I still had no idea that I was destined to follow in his oar strokes…well, almost.

Scillies came and went, and although personally memorable to both Paul and myself, for our best ever 5th finish in the men's championships, something else hung there, on the edge of thought…like a wave that was building, and was going to break at some point … probably over me!

In the life before "Mo", this was the pinnacle of our gig rowing year…The Scillies. Every week of the Summer was a different cove, beach or harbour around the coast of Cornwall, rowing, racing, a few beers and maybe a song, all leading up to the start of the new season…and The Isles Of Scilly World Championships. Although the season ended with The County Championships at Newquay, it was always Scilly we most looked forward to.

Then it happened, Scillies was over, and there we all were in the container, commonly known as our gig shed, cleaning up the boats after a very successful campaign. Most of the ladies and men's crews were there, when up came the subject of rowing The Atlantic, and I felt my heart jump a little.

"Imagine getting that close just to tip up 180 miles from the finish" someone said

"They'd rowed 2800 miles just about, but were even short of getting an official Ocean crossing, bad enough getting a "did not finish" in the race" someone else said

"You wouldn't get me out there" nearly everyone said

"Problem is, I'm a bit lost now, after watching the dots for so long and so often, slowly crossing the Atlantic, I sort of can't wait for the next race" this was me

"Don't forget there are two boys out there now, Stu and Ed, funded by some Arab prince to try and beat the Atlantic crossing record, nothing to do with Woodvale like the race we just followed" said Paul

"Really" I said, "I'll have to have a look at them"

There was a pause, before Paul said, "Does nobody fancy rowing The Atlantic?"

"No…not a chance!" came back the nearly universal response…except for one…

"Well, I know I will probably live to regret this, or perhaps I should say hopefully I will live to regret this…but yes, actually!" This was of course me, and I continued…

"I got so wrapped up in the last race, we both did, will we be happy just watching other people's dots again, when there could be the remote chance, that instead of watching the dots…we could be one!"

"Well there's the choice then," said Paul, "To wait and watch the dots again in two years…less now, or give it a go to be a dot…what do you think?"

It went very quiet in the container while people tried to decide whether we were joking or not. I picked up and looked at the print out that had been passed around, of the Atlantic route, and the coloured dots scattered all over three thousand miles of Ocean.

I looked up at Paul…and he looked back.

"I think I am going to feel very strongly annoyed with myself, if at the start of the next race, I could have been a dot, and all I am doing is watching other people's dots again…" I said. There was a pause before I said "…let's be a dot !"

"That's it then" said Paul, and all the others laughed, "Are you two serious?"

"Yes" we both said together.

"You happy to go with me ?" I said to Paul

"Yeh, course, you really want to go, I can see that, and that'll do for me"

I couldn't help but feel a bit proud, extremely excited and stupidly pleased with myself.

My heart pounded, rowing The Atlantic with Paul Harris, then a thought struck me, he's rowed all his life, I've only ever rowed gigs…and not for that long.

Suddenly a second thought hit me between the eyes…

"I can't row pair of paddles!" I said, "at least I've never done it…"

"Well, you've got three thousand miles to learn then!" was Paul's only reply!

That just leaves the tricky bit…how do I tell "The Wife??"

Crossing the line in 5th, Isles of Scilly World Gig Championships, Men's final, May 2006

The waves were already fairly big, maybe 25 feet or so, but in the warm sunshine, rowing along as best we could, close to, but annoyingly not quite exactly with the sea behind us, it was really not unpleasant. But as the sun started to go down, the shadows made the waves appear larger…darker, and altogether less appealing, if not downright unfriendly.

It was our sixth night out from La Gomera, and we were yet to have a good one, but tonight seemed the worst so far. The wind was getting up, and caught the aft cabin, slewing the boat at an awkward angle down the front of the waves, and neither of us fancied the idea of trying to keep her straight in the dark. There was the distinct possibility of being turned broadside on to the waves, which could spell disaster.

"We'll try a drogue'* said Paul, "…see if it will keep us a bit straighter down these waves."

The dusk deepened, and angry looking clouds seemed to accelerate the rapidly spreading dark. We were being buffeted by wind driving us one way, and the sea pushing us the other, and the small drogue was having no effect whatsoever. We pulled it in and attached the bigger one, letting it trail behind us on about sixty metres of rope…but the wind was too strong, catching the cabin like a sail, and turning us round, slipping and sliding down the front of the waves.

It would be completely dark soon… "We'll try the Para-Anchor…it could do with a test, see how it hangs." said Paul.

I pulled the bag containing what was effectively a twelve foot diameter parachute, out from the forward hatch, took it from its bag and handed it to Paul. He unscrewed the shackles and attached the ropes, the tripping line and the buoy rope, which should keep the para-anchor within about three metres of the surface, and threw her over the side.

The boat swung round as the anchor bit, and took hold. We watched for a few minutes, before stretching out as best we could in the aft cabin, which could cope very well with one, but with both of us in there…it was far from ideal!

We shut the hatch…it was stuffy and hot, and the solar air vents, although working, weren't able to provide enough fresh air to be comfortable, but we daren't have the hatch open even on the catch, as "Mo" had a nasty habit of suddenly, and without warning, throwing a wave or at least soaking spray right over the boat, and we couldn't risk getting the electrics or bedding wet so early in the trip. It was cramped and uncomfortable, and the heat was stifling.

The sound of the angry sea outside was deafening, and although we had been warned about this, it was much worse and louder than we ever imagined, as the waves pounded relentlessly against the sides of the cabin, like a drum. For the first hour or so, we both expected the worst…something was bound to break…a seam was bound to split, crack or burst, and at any moment we would feel cold sea water filling the cabin, such was the noise and the force of water constantly smashing into us. It felt like we were in a washing machine on boil wash, a spin drier on fast spin and a tumble drier on tumble, all at the same time.

But after the first hour, our belief grew and grew in "The Reason Why", we were still hot, cramped and uncomfortable...but we were safe!! Not a sign of any leak, crack, split or tear, and if She, and our handiwork in building her, could withstand this amount of battering by wind and waves...She could withstand anything!

I think despite the noise and conditions, we actually dozed a while, on and off, and later, our confidence growing, risked having the hatch fastened slightly open, to let in some welcome fresh air.

The boat lurched and bounced around, but defied every effort to tip Her over, and after several hours of this, we'd had enough...

"Let's have a go at rowing, pull in the para-anchor, and see what we can do. This is getting us nowhere, we can't sleep properly and if we don't get out of this cabin soon, we'll seize up!" we both felt the same, so we went out on deck, and I closed the hatch behind us as Paul made his way across the lurching boat to the bow, and the para-anchor rope.

"The buoy's gone!!" he shouted, "...the sea-anchor has sunk and it's bouncing us, trying to pull the bow under, we must get it up quick! It's gone directly under the boat...sixty metres under the boat!" (in my head, I heard Robert Shaw say " it's gone under the boat... I think it's gone under the boat!")**

"Come and grab this rope..."

We both took hold, and pulled it up, a foot or so at a time, as the boat dipped and rose on the swell. It was hellish hard to hold on to the rope as it tightened, and tried to grab back the foot or so of rope you had just struggled to pull up. As soon as it eased, we pulled up another foot or so, not daring to pull any more, as we would never have held it as it pulled back down on the swell.

Pulling that twelve foot diameter para-anchor vertically up through sixty metres of water, on to the deck of a small lurching boat...in the dark, remains as one of the most difficult things I have ever had to do, but after about 25 minutes or so, our hands throbbing and our hearts pounding, we saw the parachute anchor surface, and appear over the side of the boat.

We let out a massive sigh of relief as we collapsed on top of the mountain of wet rope and parachute that literally covered the entire deck!

We soon began to recover, realizing that we were in fact drifting without anchor or oar in the water, so we cleared a space and Paul took to the oars while I tidied up ropes and shackles, and stacked everything neatly and re-bagged the parachute, all ready to go back where they belonged when it got light.

We had at least learned an important lesson, apart from gaining complete trust in our boat, we said there and then, that unless we were being blown 180 degrees the wrong way, we would keep rowing whatever, and never put that bloody para-anchor out again...and we never did !!"

"Now keep your eyes open" said Paul, as it started to get light "see if we can find our buoy!"

* Drogue- smaller version of parachute anchor intended to slow the boat speed in a following sea.

**quote from "Jaws"

Isles of Scilly World Gig Championships, May 2007

2007 Atlantic Rowing Race

The 2007 Woodvale Atlantic Rowing Race begins on 2nd December, and will finish sometime from mid January 2008, most pairs aiming for 50 – 60 days.

As if the race itself isn't hard enough, and it *is* incredibly hard, there is a lot of truth in the old adage that says that the hardest part is getting to the start line. This usually consists, as in our case, of nearly 2 years of begging, stealing and borrowing, equipment, donations and materials for the boat, getting sponsorship and constantly fundraising, as it is not a cheap thing to do. After sorting out our chosen charity, to which all funds and proceeds from the sale of the boat upon our return will be directed, we have been training morning, noon and night, holding down our jobs to try and pay for it all, and in every other waking minute, trying to build the boat in which we hope to achieve our goal and trust with our lives. Once we are on that start line, all we have to do is row, and stay alive…well, almost!

The race starts from San Sebastian de La Gomera, in The Canary Islands, (the very harbour where Columbus set sail from on his first voyage of discovery in 1492), and crosses The Atlantic, East to West, hopefully picking up The Trade Winds on the way, as Columbus did. The finishing line is a mere 1 kilometre wide, from a line through Shirley Heights Lighthouse, at the entrance to English Harbour, Antigua. The trip is approximately 2936 miles (2552 nautical miles), but with wind and tide, most people will well exceed 3000 miles.

"Woodvale" are the race organizers, the company founded by Chay Blyth, who along with John Ridgeway in 1966, were the first successful 20th century trans Atlantic rowers. "Woodvale" is now run by Simon Chalk, himself a successful trans Atlantic and trans Indian Ocean rower, who also takes part in this 2007 renewal as a rower. Although there are two safety yachts that will patrol the fleet of 22 boats, they are for emergencies only, and the rowers must be unsupported, and receive no outside assistance, to receive a finishing position in the race. There are solo, pairs and fours race classes.

Our chosen Charity, St.Julia's Hospice Hayle, and Mount Edgcumbe Hospice St Austell, have merged to become…….

Registered Charity No. 1113

Chapter 3 – The How, When, What and Where, but no mention of Why Stages…
(…condensed to avoid too much boring detail…and in verse for fun!).

So there we stood, the deal was done
It all kicked off from here
Decision and Commitment made
For this, and all next year.

We registered with Woodvale Events
And filled in forms to pay
Then they told us they'd gone bust*
But things would be ok!

I'm glad to say they were, and now
They Woodvale Challenge became
We ordered up our boat kit pack
But what would be Her name?

We thought "The Oiled Cormorant"
Or "Buttered Pig" might fly?
But then "Trelawny's Navy"** led us
To "The Reason Why".

We chose our local Charity
Of Cornwall Hospice Care
We said we'd raise some cash for them
Which they thought very fair.

Bank accounts were opened
A hundred letters sent
But we didn't get the money back
That we on postage spent!

Rebecca*** drew the logo
The wave of T.R.Y.
T-shirts and polo's all designed
For everyone to buy.

Interviews on radio
And photos in the press
But whether people heard or read
Was anybody's guess.

Necklaces and key rings from
St.Justin****, then we knew
We'd have to build the boat
To show them what we said was true!

Sponsors stickers printed
The pack of ply arrives
But can we glue it well enough
For us to stake our lives?

Resin and Epoxy
Fibreglass and glue
Plywood wedges, cable ties and
Paint gold, white and blue.

Fundraisers at weekends
And full time work all day
With boatbuilding most every night
There was no time to play.

Autumn turned to Winter
And an all too common sight
Was us upon our rowing machines
Before the Dawn's first light.

The website kept expanding
It takes all Jennie's***** time
But money from our sponsors starts
The mountainside to climb.

Buy a square for just a pound
Or guess the time we'll take
A mountain bike and fifty quid
The prizes for the stake.

Suddenly our plywood stack
Takes shape into a boat
And the only doubt we have to check
Is will She really float?

Stainless Steel and bolts and ropes
Sliding seats and catches
High tech stuff, but will we get
Our backsides through the hatches?

Batteries Gel, and solar panels
A Navigation light
GPS and AIS******
For Tankers in the night!

We launched Her on St.Patrick's Day
Our genius master plans
From Penzance Slip to Guinness
In the bar at "Flanagans"*******

She slowly off the trailer slid
Our precious baby boat
All fears and worries gone like that
As She sat silently afloat.

But so badly did She dip and roll
As we both climbed aboard
We both looked scared and said aloud
"We'll leave the blighter moored!"

But oars in place and gates******** screwed up
It made a splendid sight
As we flew across The Harbour
Like a buttered pig in flight!

Her maiden voyage over
Off to "Flanagans" for beer
Raising money and a glass
In St.Patrick's Day good cheer.

The months that followed quickly passed
With fitting all the bits
Gas cooker, stainless lifelines and
The mother of first aid kits!

The anchor was no problem
But what became a pain
Was finding space enough to stow
A four and a half mile chain!********

Easter at The Tinners Arms *********
BBQ's at The Gurnards Head
We tried "The Ginger Tosser"
And put "Betty Stoggs" to bed!

Raising funds, and carnivals
Filled all our Summer days
The clock was ticking fast as we
Began the final phase.

One training day to Mousehole
One more across Mounts Bay
Across the surf on Hayle bar
And we'd be on our way.

Then came all the courses
Radio, VHF
But would anyone be near enough
Is anybody's guess.

First Aid with poor old Annie**********
Needing CPR we knew
And if wounded by a biro
We would both know what to do!

Then came sea survival
In a swimming pool was tough
Getting in and righting life rafts
When those pool waves were so rough!

Last was Ocean yacht master
Navigation by the sun
A week of calculation
Put our tiny brains on stun.

But to find our true horizon
And our zenith overhead
We didn't take a sextant but
A GPS instead.

And so the Summer faded
Website countdown ticked away
A forty-eight hour training row
And we would be ok.

Desalination water makers
Concept oars to row
Stick the number on the bow
And we were set to go!

Buying one way tickets
On the internet machine
Planes, hotels and Islands where
I'm sure I've never been.

Dried food arrived in boxes
Enough for forty two
And two more trips to Tesco meant
That this would have to do.

We crammed the boat, and fully packed
She soon was Newark bound
A whole adventure on its own***********
When P.A. Freight we found.

That was it, our time was over
Farewell alone remains
For La Gomera calls to us
By trains and boats and planes.

The time for prep was done and gone
The time for action here
And we were ready for the task...
Well...once we'd drunk our beer.

Key.

 * The company organizing the race was Woodvale Events Ltd, who went into receivership over a previous failed venture. It was extremely worrying, that after parting with several thousand pounds between us, we were told not to pay any more to Woodvale Events Ltd, who were now in receivership, and we could lose our money. Happily, the receiver thought the 2007 race and the assets of the Woodvale group, mainly boats and the expected entry fees etc. were enough to let the monies paid, be transferred to a new company, Woodvale Challenge Ltd. Who would now administer the race. Everyone restarted payments to them, and no money was lost.

** While sitting at the water's edge one day, between Newlyn and Mousehole, notebook in hand trying to think of a suitable name for our new Ocean rowing boat, I was trying to get an angle on Trelawny's Army, the inspirational Cornish Anthem. As I sat there, the Penlee Lifeboat came roaring by, the wash hitting the rock I was sitting on, soaking me and "Baggins" my dog. Suddenly, Trelawny's Navy came into my head, and the chorus line, "The Reason Why". I excitedly text Paul, who text me back, "Perfect, that'll do for me".

***Rebecca, my daughter, designed the stylized wave symbol, from the conjoined letters of T, R and Y. for "The Reason Y". Have a look at the bottom of the page.

**** St.Justin, a Celtic Jewellery company whose owner, Jeremy Gilbert, rowed with us over the years, and was part of the 5th place crew of 2006. They kindly commissioned pewter necklaces and key rings for "The Reason Why" to sell.

***** Jennie Richards, the third member of "The Reason Why" team, shore based, Jennie organized donations and ran the blogs and the website, was our first point of contact during the race, and was generally invaluable.

****** Satellite navigation and Radar equiptment

******* "Flanagans" Irish bar in Penzance, who sponsored us, sadly now gone.

******** These are rowing gates that screw tight, and keep the oars in place.

********* Mandatory equipment, according to Woodvale checklist, included a chain and anchor! In some parts the Atlantic was over four and a half miles deep!! Of course it was for start or finish, not mid ocean, especially if we hit the wrong end of Antigua.

**********The Tinners Arms and The Gurnards Head, my local pubs in Zennor, who both supported us. Ginger Tosser and Betty Stoggs, both beers from Skinners brewery.

*********** "Annie" is the Dummy we all had to practice CPR on, 1st aid course.

************ The trip to the shipping company, P.A.Freight to deliver "The Reason Why" for onward shipping to La Gomera, was an adventure all on its own, and an account of it is included in the "Pre Race blog" later.

I haven't said much about the endless, tedious, mind numbing hours on the rowing machine, running the cliff path, circuit training in the gym etc. I didn't want to be reminded! Suffice to say, we did it, and for me, it was a 1-2 hour rowing machine, and cliff jog, before work, often in the dark, every day for 18 months, plus gym and rowing at nights after work.

Now you may have thought, that being ripped unceremoniously away from all normality…my normality that is…and everyone I hold dear, was enough of a trauma for one small pig to bear, but no…

You may have thought that being ungraciously re-christened "Droops", (what sort of name is that anyway?), and having it written in permanent marker on my soft pink under belly, was undignified enough, but no…

And you surely would have thought that being mercilessly super glued to the roof of the aft cabin of a 23 foot long rowing boat, about to embark on the madness of a Trans Atlantic Rowing Race, exposed to every element imaginable, and being in constant fear of being washed away, when I wasn't in constant fear of being continually squeezed to be made to oink that is, was humiliating enough, and at worse downright dangerous enough, but no…

…there was more to follow…

At a time that appeared to me to be completely the same as any other, by way of the surroundings, sea, sky, night, day, sunshine, rain, wind or calm, but which these two rowing twits, who I am now convinced are as mad as cheese, suddenly decided to call "Christmas", whatever that is, then decided to wrap tinsel round my neck!

So now they sit around muttering about how strange "Christmas" is this year, and it is at this point, that it is all I can do to stop me saying, " O…is it really you pair of numpties!" "You want to try and look at it from where I am for a bit, sitting there drinking rum." Do they offer me a sip?…what do you think?

It's all I can do not to continually sneeze, with this tinsel tickling my snout!

O for some lovely sticky black mud…

I wasn't awake, and sat almost semi stunned, having part crawled and part dragged myself to the rowing seat in the bow. What am I doing here?...Why did Paul wake me up?... Where was Paul going?...Why was he shutting the hatch and leaving me out here on my own?...I can't do it on my own I thought, not tonight, I feel too weak and I need to go back to sleep.

He threw one final look up at me before the hatchway closed. I tried desperately to think of something to say to make him keep it open…but my mind was befuddled, and not a word came out…then it was shut. Ten feet away but it may as well have been ten miles.

I felt dejected, utterly miserable and alone.

Why couldn't I see anything? Where was The Grinning Turk?*

It was inky black and an extremely choppy, big, unfriendly sea, with quite a wind blowing behind it…making it angry… which was trying to constantly make the boat turn side on to the waves. It was not comfortable, not easy to row, and not at all pleasant. What the hell was I doing here, I thought yet again.

Eventually, as my fuzzy head began to clear, courtesy of having cold sea water thrown constantly and violently in my face, I realised that to make the boat go in the direction I wanted, and to stop being blown and bounced all over The Atlantic, I would have to, and this may have been obvious to some, pick up the oars and row!

I slowly turned the boat around, and started to row in roughly the right direction, as near as I could make out at least, as the compass light was not clear or very bright, but "Orion" and "The Plough" were roughly in their right places in the sky for me to be going the right way, and it was then I made a remarkable discovery. For once, the wind and waves seemed to be behind me, blowing and pushing me the way I wanted to go. This was unusual but very welcome on this night.

I thought I could see a light on the horizon behind me…I blinked and stared hard, my tired eyes not focusing properly, and the big sea blotting out the horizon for minutes at a time. But there it was…a light…bigger than a few minutes ago, if only that lazy Turk was up I might be able to see better. Wow…that's one hell of a ship, and it's really flying judging by how big the light on it is getting.

I briefly thought of having a panic, why hadn't the "Sea me" or "AIS" radar alarms gone off? Has Paul turned them off …again, so it wouldn't wake him up… again?

I must have been waking up a little by now, because I began to reason, "That light is too big for a ship…and why is there a cloud in front of it?"

"What a pratt!" I shouted out loud, it's him, the long lost Grinning Turk just coming up over the horizon…I laughed out loud "What a plonker!"

Less than an hour later, climbing up the sky, the Grinning Turk shone the most beautiful moonlight trail across the ocean, in almost the exact path we were travelling, and all I had to do was to stay on it.

No longer hurtling backwards into the inky void, I was skimming majestically across the silvery surface of a watery moonlit trail with consummate ease.

It was another world...another time...another life... and as if planned to order, I picked up my I-Pod, which I had forgotten about, as the first few bars of "Stairway to Heaven" floated from the earpiece, out across the deck...it was perfect!

The night sky welcomed the sound with open arms, the sea seemed to calm slightly, and the wind seemed to drop just a tad as the waves began to roll in time to the rhythm. The wind carried the tune on its wings until it seemed it was humming the melody.

The Grinning Turk grinned even brighter, as he climbed higher in the night sky, smiling down on us all, moving along in harmony, as if in a dream.

* "The Grinning Turk" – The Moon...the first time we saw him, he came up with a cloud across his face, making him look at first, like The Holy Grail Chalice, but afterwards, he became more like a cartoon Saracen Prince with an enormous grinning smile. This soon evolved, and he quickly became "The Grinning Turk."

Chapter 4 – The Pre Race Blog

29th September 2006

Today, we took delivery of "The Reason Why", although there was no sign of a boat, just a pile of plywood. Many thanks to Torridge Transport for delivering it, Billy Faull for unloading it, and Alan Baumbach for providing the shed in which to build it. Now all we have to do is put it together, it can't be that difficult...can it?

4th October 2006

Having cut out all the various pieces of wood, the job of gluing them together began – cable ties came in very handy to keep everything in place until dry.

7th October 2006

Do you remember the days when your parents bought you "Airfix" kits for Christmas? Well this is much the same thing, sort of … only bigger. Suffice to say the gluing continues! The middle section can be seen in the background of one of the following photos, leant up against the wall. The photo shows us working on the bow.

10th October 2006

Over the last week, we have spent most evenings and the weekend gluing the various parts of the boat together. We did this in three separate sections, and then joined these together to form the basis of the boat. During this time Steve was contacted by Radio Cornwall, to do an interview about the trip, and hopefully this will have raised local awareness, which may result in further sponsorship.

14th October 2006

Today we started putting the bottom sections onto the main framework…it is now starting to look something like a boat.

29th October 2006

Two phrases sum up the current situation- "relentless resin-ing" and "eternal epoxy-ing".

11th November 2006

The sides and front cabin have been planked. The deck has also been covered, leaving access holes to the storage areas below.

22nd November 2006

You can see the sleeping compartment, (aft cabin), complete with roof and hatch hole. You can see the view from our bedroom as well!

16th December 2006

The resin-ing has been completed, and the whole boat is currently undergoing wet and dry sanding, in preparation for the first coat of paint, which is scheduled to be done next week.

31st December 2006

The last day of 2006, and so far "The Reason Why" has had two coats of undercoat, some of the hatches in the rear cabin have been installed, and the waterline marked on in pencil.

The above six photos are the result of about three weeks work…Happy New Year!

7th January 2007

The first photos of 2007, and during the Christmas holidays, the bottom of the boat has had its first coat of black paint, and the sides have been painted blue. Contrary to the beliefs of the "Devoran 4", this shade of blue is called "Zennor Blue" and definitely not "Devoran Blue!" No doubt comments will be posted on the guestbook drekkly! Ha Ha.

20th January 2007

One of us got a bit carried away with some yellow paint – the boat looked awful! So, over the last ten days, we have been experimenting with new colour schemes, and all but reinstating the paintwork of nearly two weeks ago! The name has been painted on, the runners have been fixed to the deck, and some of the hatches have now been installed.

1st February 2007

The following photos show the seating positions either side of the boat, and the sleeping cabin, which looks fairly spacious in the first photo, but add a couple of rowers and it soon becomes very cosy!

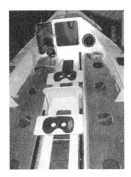 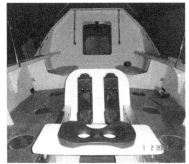 

15th February 2007

The cabin now has a map of the world sticker placed on the side, and the hatch has been installed in the cabin roof. Lots of small jobs continue to be completed each week, which are too numerous to mention

25th February 2007

The red and black, waterproof hatch covers have now been added, which give access to the storage areas below deck. The deck itself has been painted with non-skid paint. Work continues on the rudder and the foot rests.

We are working very hard to get everything ready for the launch day, I cannot believe I just wrote that, but yes, 17th March 2007, St. Patrick's Day, has been set for the launch, and anything we haven't done before it, will have to be done after.

I can't tell you how difficult that map of the World sticker was, don't look too closely, I've ripped Florida! And there's one on the other side as well with a crease through Europe!

Our labour of love is nearing completion, and what a beautiful thing she is

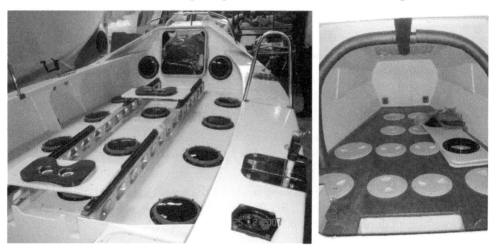

SATURDAY 17TH MARCH 2007, ST.PATRICKS DAY...and THE LAUNCH

Sailing Club Slipway, Penzance.

"The Reason Why" was blessed by Rev. Brin Berriman of St.Buryan, formerly of Zennor

The moment of truth, would she float ...

In the centre above, is Sue Harvey, from Cornwall Hospice Care, our Charity.

"Cornish" oars, kindly loaned by Chris Barrett and Bob Warren-"Spirit of Cornwall"

I might well scratch my head…I was supposed to be rowing

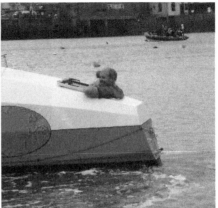

As you can see, everyone has their strengths…Paul's is rowing……………….

There are no photos of the after launch party in "Flanagans"…which is probably just as well on reflection! Suffice to say, that after we downed 4 pints of Guinness each to get a very silly green Leprechaun hat, we decided to try and get one for the entire gig crew! Which was almost certainly even sillier, but we needed to bulk up, well that was the excuse!

One day this would become "The Bearpit"…and on show at Falmouth

Since the launch day, we have been fitting more equipment. Mattresses for the sleeping compartment, sectional so we can access the storage hatches below, solar panels only a few millimeters thick on the aft cabin roof, which will, apparently charge the two gel batteries shown below, and keep us powered up for the whole trip…well, that's the plan. We have fitted the cooker, which is on a "gimble" so it stays level and upright even in rough seas. We have two positions for this, higher as shown below, next to the aft cabin hatch, and lower in the foot well, under the aft cabin hatch. Then there is the most vital piece of equipment on the boat, and one of the single most expensive, upon which, after the boat, our lives would depend, this is of course the water maker. We took advice and decided to get what most experts agreed was the best, a "Spectra Ventura", I think it was called. At £3000, nearly as expensive as the boat, I haven't thanked every donation individually here, but special mention must go to Paul's brother Terry, for the water maker, And well done Paul for successfully fitting it, breaking his rule of a lifetime, and actually opening the instruction booklet!

We rarely cooked with the cooker in the position shown, it proved more successful lower down in the foot well. The water maker took up the entire compartment, and had to be kept dry from seawater! The gel batteries were fixed low down in position, in a compartment just inside the aft cabin floor. The orange bar seen above is the restrainer

9th April 2007

The Reason Why was taken to The Tinners Arms, Zennor, on Easter Monday, where funds were raised by selling T-Shirts, Polo Shirts and squares on a board to win a mountain bike (donated by Cycle Logic of Helston) and Guess the time we will take to get to Antigua. We also put out strategically placed donation buckets.

27th May 2007

Been too busy fitting the fiddly bits on the boat, which don't look a lot, but are time consuming, we now have an array of aerials, and the electrics are all installed.

9th June 2007

The Reason Why complete with sponsors stickers and logos and a new trailer, courtesy of Tyrone Snell, was on display at Gyllingvase Beach Falmouth, at the gig event. It provoked a lot of interest and raised more funds, and our profile for the Atlantic row, now less than six months away. More worryingly, this was my wedding anniversary, but as I'm still here to tell the tale, I must have remembered ok!

July 2007

Sorry for lack of updates, you haven't missed anything. It's all been about the trouble with oars! Are they the right ones, and if they are, why don't they fit the rowing gates? Anyway, all ok now. Through "Concept" we have had feedback from no less than James Cracknell, and if they're ok for him, then they're ok for us!

Friday 27th July 2007 – The mandatory 48 hour row

Departed Mylor slipway for Woodvale mandatory 48hr. row. Half an hour in, first encounter with two enormous ships, exiting Falmouth harbour, the Harbour Pilot was quite precise in his instructions to us, it was " get out the f…ing way", which we understood fully, and removed ourselves forthwith!

We visited St. Anthony's Lighthouse, had a cup of tea, just to test the cooker, and crossed the bay to the mouth of The Helford River, where we moored up for a while. We set off for a night row to Dodman Point, the GPS said it was 14.7 miles, and we started fine, but by 2245 ish, the wind started to pick up from the South-West, and we feared we wouldn't get back against it if we went any further. We had rowed 7.5 miles, but the 7.5 miles back into the still increasing wind took 4.5 hours, and it was hard work. Not to mention our 2nd and 3rd close encounters with super tankers, but let me tell you, they are infinitely more scary at night! We did manage to avoid them though, but you can't imagine how busy the mouth of Carrick Roads is, and we were glad to get across it, even though it did seem to take forever.

As we slowly drew back into the sheltered mouth of The Helford, it was 0330 hrs. and we found a few hours sleep at anchor, fairly easy!

Saturday 28th July 2007

Breakfasted and refreshed, we set off to The Manacles, Porthoustock actually, for the local gig racing event, which we watched at anchor, before running back to Falmouth, trying to stay ahead of the forecast heavy rain on its way. Blackrock Buoy seemed an awful long way and the mouth to Carrick Roads was chopping up nastily, as the rain inevitably caught us up, and we were soaked through to the skin way before we got there. At one point, we were going 2.6 knots in the wind without rowing, and we realized then, just what a difference having a friendly wind can make.

It was horrible as we tried to put on dry clothes, and cook a meal, even in the relative shelter of The Truro River, where we now were. But even here, the wind gusted strongly all night.

Sunday 29th July

It dawned raining, but cleared up nicely as we rowed back up The Truro River and into Carrick Roads, round and about the inlets and the boats, timed just right for 1200 hours, and the end of our 48 hour row. But timed just about as wrong as you can get in Mylor Harbour, as there was no water at the slipway, to recover The Reason Why! We had to float her on to the trailer in the water, She was no gig, and far too heavy to lift on our own. Not only that, there was that damned blue Devoran gig blocking up the slipway as well!

Joking aside, a big thank you to Devoran Gig Club, for giving us a lift and helping recover the boat, just as well they were there really. An especially big thank you to Nicky for gratuitously splashing water in my face when at my most vulnerable, but then could I expect anything more?

Porthoustock… training!

But still, we had been out for 48 hours on the boat, found out about oars, electrics, cooking, night rowing, headwinds and "The Bucket". (Obviously with no toilet, or heads on board, the system was known as "Bucket and Chucket!"). Talking of leaks, apart from a small rain drip through a couple of bolts, the boat went great, and we had rowed 42 miles, only about 2900 miles less than the row we're training for!

Getting near the sharp end now, as the boat is due to be shipped to La Gomera in two months or so. Let's hope the forest fires of La Gomera and The Canaries in general, have stopped burning by then - for all the people living there, not just The Atlantic Rowing Race.

We'll keep you posted with whatever happens between now and then.

Sunday 26th August 2007 – The Gurnards Head Hotel, Zennor

Many thanks to Charlie and Andy, and all staff at The Gurnards, for hosting a Summer Barbeque in the garden, overlooking the stunning Zennor scenery, and donating a barrel of Betty Stoggs Bitter, and the food. The event was very well supported and raised £600 towards our Charity, Cornwall Hospice Care.

The Gurnards Head Barbeque. I'm not sure if Charles (the owner) has his head in his hands because of the beer he's donating, or if it's because he's trying to get Roger (who he's talking to) to come back and finish the work he started in 2002!

Special thanks to Chunky and Roger Warren, and everyone else for their donations. For the record, there is no truth in the rumour that one potential ocean rower, tried his best, but failed miserably, to drink dry, the barrel of Betty Stoggs bitter!! The three happy faces in the aft hatchway are Amy and Sam Oliver, with Paul's daughter Danielle. The intense discussion at the bow, possibly about rowing, but more probably about who's round it was, is between George and Jeremy.

Bank Holiday Monday, 27th August 2007 – Newlyn Fish Festival

The following day of this busy weekend, we took T.R.Y. to The Fish Festival at Newlyn. Hopefully raising the profile of our forthcoming adventure, and raising over £300 in the process. By the end of the day, the head had finally cleared, and we were questioned out, and we could have done with a tape recorder, as everybody seemed to ask the same things, "How long will it take?" "When are you going?" "Where are you going from?" "Where's that?" "Why are you leaving in winter?" "Are you going to row back?" "What size are the engines?" (Seriously!!), "Are you mad?" Of course, the answer to the last question is possibly still in the balance!

31st August 2007

Have been out in the boat a few more times now, but there always seems to be a strong headwind, and the coastline around here doesn't take prisoners. If the wind is right, then inevitably the tide isn't, to launch after work, and it seems even more unreliable at weekends. We did manage a trip from Penzance towards Lamorna, past Mousehole, but again, all too soon, a strong head wind appeared and made progress difficult. We tried our 1 hour on and 1 hour off rowing routine for a while, but soon the wind dictated that we tested the sea anchor again. Strange to say, that not only did it hold our position, but it caught the outgoing tide and current, and actually pulled us out against the wind faster than we had been able to row into it! This is an important point to remember, when it is more efficient to deploy the sea anchor and save energy, and still make progress.

Also had a trip out, across the notorious Hayle Bar to St. Ives, this went well and the wind was kind to us for a change. The strangest thing was the hot air balloon that appeared very low over St.Ives, and slowly drifted over the Hayle Estuary. Mental note, for training, put more weight/ballast in the boat, still sitting a bit high and light.

September 2007

The Reason Why joined the three Zennor Cornish Pilot Gigs, Senara, Morvoren and Melusine, to take part in the Zennor Carnival, in September. It has to be said, that having a route of only 1.5 miles, means the walking entrants in their fancy dress, dictate the speed of the vehicles…slow. This year however, in yet another example of Health and Safety gone mad, we were forced to have traffic management(a policeman in squad car), which involved the said policeman telling us we couldn't have anyone walking the route, and all the floats had to follow him in his squad car. He then proceeded to zoom off at 50 mph, from The Gurnards Head to The Tinners Arms in the village, and thus he had created the fastest carnival in history, the procession lasting all of 5 minutes!! It only lasted 5 minutes because I stopped and held up everyone behind me. It was a bit of a joke, still we did get to the bar quicker than we expected!

Zennor Carnival, September 2007

17th October 2007

Well, as the website now proudly displays (thanks Jen), only 45 days 10 hours 51 minutes and 2 seconds to the start of the race on 2nd December. Things are coming together fairly well, and last night, Paul and I ran through the entire Woodvale inventory/checklist, and it would appear we have everything…amazing!

Talk about a mountain of stuff. It will be like trying to get a pint into a half pint pot, when we pack it all in the boat tonight. As for the food, it looks like we have enough to feed an army for a year, but having to take a mandatory 90 day supply, has inflated the food to a veritable mountain of black bin liners, full of daily ration packs of "just add water" or "boil in a bag", we have both, of muesli, pasta, rice, noodles, go bars, chilli con carne, spaghetti bolognaise, crisps, peanuts, curry and the inevitable pot noodles, the first item on the menu of international cuisine! It will be pot luck which ration bag we pick each day, and one day's delight of chicken curry and chocolate chip mousse, may well be countered by the next day's wolf fish and a bag of raisins! (What the hell is wolf fish anyway?).

Rowing duo take on the Atlantic

FROM LEFT: STEVE GARDNER, SPONSOR JOHN WOMBWELL AND PAUL HARRIS

Photo from "Cornwall Today" showing my boss, John Wombwell. Without his support and generosity, I could never have gone, so I owe him a big debt of gratitude. Thanks John.

The last items on the equipment list, were the Satellite phone SIM card, and the truly massive first aid kit! (There's stuff in there that Doc Martin would need to look up what they were for!) These we have now purchased, thanks to the ladies darts team from The Globe Inn, Lostwithiel, who did a 24 hour darts marathon, and raised a fantastic £1300 for us and Cornwall Hospice Care. Thanks to Will in The Globe, and Georgina, Michele, Tina, Angela, Marion, Jeannie, Maisey and especially Karen for organizing it all...it was a great success.

We have been out rowing in T.R.Y again, for a night row out from Penzance to Mountamopus Buoy off Cudden Point and back, about 8-9 miles, just a little loosener.

One thing I should add, is the board of 1000 squares we have been selling for a mountain bike, kindly donated by Cycle Logic of Helston, has been drawn. The winning number was 440, and the winner is Lydia Dean-Barrows, from St. Ives. Paul and I will be presenting the bike to Lydia very soon. Well, there you have it, the early morning rowing machine hour, and running the cliff path in the dark stage is nearly over, and together with the endless fundraising and begging letters, we are nearly there.

On Friday 19th October, Paul and I deliver The Reason Why, fully packed and ready to go, to the freight company in Newark (Nottingham), for shipping to La Gomera. Soon after, on 20th November, it will be Paul and I that ship ourselves out on trains, planes, automobiles and ferries (one better than Steve Martin!), on one way tickets, to rejoin the fruit of our labours, and trusty wooden steed "The Reason Why" in The Canaries.

A big thank you to everyone who has helped, donated, and supported us, which has enabled us to get where we are now...so very close now to that elusive start line.

A massive thank you to Simon at Hotdog, Lostwithiel, for all the vinyl's, stickers, T-shirts etc. I promise that's the lot now...well...probably?!

Look at that, writing this, with a thousand interruptions, the clock says 45 days, 8 hours, 58 minutes and 42 seconds to go. Doesn't time just fly!

Lydia Dean-Barrows receiving the mountain bike from us in The Gurnards Head.

Friday 19th October

So there we were driving back from Newark (yes, north of Nottingham), having dropped off The Reason Why for shipping to La Gomera (She was going from Felixstowe...we couldn't work it out either). But these were the experts, we'd been told, they had done it all before and they had the precision purpose made cradles that would carry our precious boats safely and securely, from lorry, dock and ship, to the quay at La Gomera.

Mind you, after 3 hours (the 2 girls in front of us had been there 5 hours!), of watching lads scour the weeds and undergrowth around the perimeter of the P.A Freight car park, looking for nasty pieces of weather stained wood with nails sticking out of them, some with faded names of boats from The Atlantic Rowing Race 2 years ago, still attached to them with rusty drawing pins, we began to have our doubts. They then proceeded to nail these pieces of wood together, on top of each other with 6 inch nails. Surely these weren't the precision and purpose made cradles that we had driven so far in the wrong direction, and paid so much for? It soon became apparent however, that they were!

We looked at each other with disbelief, but what could we do now, we were stuck with it. The clincher was being asked to help turn the girls boat around, as it was the wrong way for the cradle, now nailed together to a scrap pallet with a bit of pipe lagging! We looked doubtful, but did as asked. We then watched as old, frayed strops, that were far too long, were coiled round and around themselves on the forks of a very large forklift truck. After several attempts, the boat was lifted and positioned ready to lower on to the purpose made cradle (we knew this, as we had spent 2 hours watching it being purpose made), when, as Paul had said to me almost at once, the chap driving the forklift stopped, deliberated for a few minutes, and the announced that the boat was the wrong way round! As suspected, it was right in the first place. So he began to unload the boat, get us to turn it around again to try again. Paul, being a very practical chap, along with a young lad who was helping, both stopped the driver and suggested, "why don't you turn the bloody cradle round, you've got umpteen forklifts?" Finally, this is what he did.

We were convinced that the so called security cameras that were all over the place, were actually "Beadles About", or "You've been Framed", it just had to be a joke, they were just seeing how much we would take, before they would jump out and surprise us...unfortunately not!

So, having left our pride and joy, with these "experts", there we were, mid Friday afternoon, trying to drive home from Newark, towing an empty 40 foot gig trailer, on a day that the press later christened "Black Friday". It was the worst traffic I'd ever seen, and all we had to do, was get home via the M1, M6, M42, M5, and A30, which were all like car parks!!

So not the best day, but the boat had gone...somewhere, we don't know where, as three weeks later, no-one seems to be able to tell us where she is, whether she has been shipped, whether she has arrived at La Gomera, or sent to Australia instead!!

In fairness, I must add a postscript, in that "The Reason Why," despite all our fears, did arrive safely in La Gomera, with only a couple of minor scratches.

16th November 2007

This was it, our last day at work! Our i-pods have been fully loaded with music and talking books, our minds are full of secret plans to melt down those damned rowing machines upon our return to Cornwall, and it is hard to believe that this day is actually here! Beer, baguettes and pasties, for lunch, then it was "farewell, and see you in February!" Once again, our thanks go to Western Power Distribution and Wombwell Homes, our two employers, without whom, we would never have been able to even start this rowing challenge.

At night, it was the first farewell party, at The Bucket of Blood, in Phillack, complete with more pasties, courtesy of Western Power, thanks again. There was a fantastic turn out from our friends, for which we were very grateful. My weekend was already brilliant, as my eldest daughter Sam, and boyfriend Alex, had made a surprise visit to see me off, having made the long drive down from Edinburgh. This meant a lot to me, to be able to say farewell to my complete family, Chris, Rebecca, Oliver, and Sam and Alex... as well as Baggins the dog!

18th November 2007

Following the great success of last Fridays farewell party, we decided to have a second one, a fantastic day at The Gurnards Head Hotel, Zennor, who kindly donated another barrel of beer, and "roasties" on the bar, another big thank you to them.

Thanks also to all the Zennor gig club members who came, The Walkers And Talkers Society, Vanessa for the cake, Andy Finch for the udder cream...a nice thought, Anne and Simon for the letters to be opened on route, Jen for the photo album duly signed by all our fellow gig rowers, cards, free beer and countless other gifts that descended upon us so generously, thank you all.

We also presented the mountain bike to Lydia, see photo previous. Thanks to everyone who bought a square. We cannot thank all our friends and families enough for their kind words and support over the past 2 years...but thanks anyway. Special thanks to our families who are about to see us go off on our adventure, our thoughts and love are with you, and don't worry, we will be back...we do not intend missing out on a truly memorable and momentous reunion party in Antigua!

Farewell party no. 2 in The Gurnards Head Hotel, Zennor, 18th November 2007

The night was as black as pitch, heavy clouds blocked out the stars, and there was no Turk...grinning or otherwise.

Something fluttered over me, not far above my head, but quick as I looked up, whatever it was had gone, swallowed by the black night.

At night, the navigation light on the boat, created a pale bubble of light around us, like our own little world in which the boat hung, motionless...the bubble that is, not the boat, which is NEVER motionless. Beyond the edge of the "bubble" was another world outside of our knowledge, thought or understanding. It was a world of dark violent winds and giant hostile waves that tried relentlessly to break into our safe little oasis of relative calm.

There it was again, fluttering above my head, it was a bird, a smallish brown thrush sized bird, but with bigger wings, that seemed to be working out whether it was a good idea to land on top of the cabin, the deck, my head, or indeed at all! I followed it in and out of our bubble world as it circled us again and again. Suddenly, we had a Tom and Jerry moment as the little bird bounced off the aft cabin roof, hit the deck, and tumbled head over tails twice, and landed in a dishevelled heap, looking straight up at me with a look on his face that clearly said, "What did you do that for?" and despite my slight concern for his well being, I had to laugh out loud.

When Paul got up, he picked him up and put him in a better place for a take off, we thought, though he showed no inclination to do so at present. Some two hours later, after I had my break and was back rowing, the little bird began to move and flap the odd wing, until without further warning he flew off, seemingly none the worse for the experience.

This was our first meeting, with who I had immediately christened "Pete The Petrel".

After this first contact, Pete became a regular, and pretty much a daily visitor. And I mean daily, every day for the rest of the trip, but despite a couple of close calls, he never landed, or crashed, on "The Reason Why" again.

There are those sceptics who will say that Pete had a little help from some of his more Westerly cousins, and had passed the baton to them, but we believe it was always Pete who kept with us all the way. We often marvelled at his ability to survive in this watery desert, thousands of miles from any land whatsoever, and although he did a very cute little twinkle toes walking on the water thing, you just had to see, we never actually saw him land on the sea either.

Pete became our constant companion, we looked forward to seeing him each day, and he never let us down. Mind you, as we got a bit nearer the domain of those beastly great Frigate Birds, he did give them a bit of a wide berth, and I don't blame him.

I've never been surfing...never been to sea...never been on the sea...well actually I've never been on a boat before!

Some of you may think this is not surprising, given that I am a small pink plastic pig, and being 1000 miles from land, Mid-Atlantic, with my trotters super glued to the top of a small wooden rowing boat, is not a naturally tenable situation for a pig...plastic or otherwise!

However, here I am, and today is another first for me, as I seem to be on an extreme, and I mean extremely extreme sort of roller coaster.

Now nobody likes a trough more than me, preferably full of food, and the bigger the better, but out here the troughs are an entirely different matter. Between the waves, if you can call them waves, the troughs are so deep and distant, they appear as far away alpine valleys, complete with imagined villages, fields and Swiss Chalets. Tiny specks on the edge of sight from our vantage point that could only be on the peaks of The Alps, far above the snow line.

Immense and enormous are words that come to mind, and then it's all change, as the trough comes up to meet us, as we fall off the edge of the world into the abyss. We are on the floor of the valley, and giant, dark and forbidding mountain peaks tower above us, and must surely crash down on top of us, swallowing us as specks of dust in a desert sand storm...but no...they just row on, into the trough, over the peaks, and once more down the other side, where more alpine valleys and mountain peaks await. It becomes dark as we reach the valley floor, with mighty walls of water rising up either side of us, leaving a strip of sky far above, fifty...sixty feet waves, I don't know but at least that, and here comes another one roaring, rolling up from behind, it must swamp us this time...but no. They just row on, and here we are on top of the world, looking down into the valley once more.

These rolling, moving mountainsides of water, seemingly in perpetual motion are almost like giant creatures... indomitable...unstoppable, travelling endlessly across thousands of miles of the vast and empty tracts of "MO"...there, they've got me saying it now. The Mighty Atlantic I'll call her, I could shorten it to "MA", with the utmost respect of course. Yes "MA" will be good, in the hope She will look after me like one!

Chapter 5 – La Gomera...the End of the Beginning!

It was a cold, wet Tuesday...**20th November 2007**, truly the longest day!!

Everything we needed, was packed in the boat already in La Gomera, or at least we hoped so, as nobody from Woodvale, the race organizers, or P.A.Freight, the shipping company, could confirm the exact whereabouts of "The Reason Why". All we had were passports, tickets and money, and there was nothing left to do but wait until the 10pm train left Penzance tonight.

I even attempted a final pull on the rowing machine, but luckily, Paul's day was dragging in the same way as mine, and he came round and we had a coffee and a chat instead.

Eventually the time arrived...the waiting and all the preparations of the last 2 years were over, and there we were, on a very cold and wet Penzance Station platform, in flip flops, with no luggage, and one way train and plane tickets.

There were the last minute hugs and kisses goodbye to Chris and Rebecca (Oliver was working and Sam had gone back to Edinburgh with Alex after their surprise weekend visit), and Paul doing the same with Dawn, Jake and Danielle. As we boarded the train, Rebecca handed me a small Bible and prayer book, and asked me to take it with me. This touched me deeply, and giving her a final hug, I said "of course I will." Then the doors were shut, and we were gone.

It felt very strange, as the sudden realisation hit us, that the way home was by way of Tenerife, La Gomera, Antigua and the small matter of 3000 miles of The Atlantic Ocean in a 23 foot rowing boat.

We drank out of date Budweiser, and feasted on in date Pringles all through the night, until after a few dozes, we reached Reading... unfortunately Reading was shut, but the Gatwick Express was on time, and although cold, it got us through the chill hour before dawn, to Gatwick, right on time, and after a full English breakfast at "Garfunkels", we were ready to fly.

 Not before having my first disaster of the trip, when somewhere between breakfast and the departure lounge, my favourite sunglasses, that I'd been wearing all summer, fell to bits! Paul had given them to me, so it wasn't the cost, but I'd gotten attached to them...had them broken in. I felt like a snooker player that broke his cue, the day before The Crucible tournament. I scanned the tiled floors of the entire terminal building, everywhere, right back to our breakfast table, nothing, the black plastic nose rest bit in the middle had gone, no doubt brushed up by one of the countless league of nations cleaning teams that swept by every 42 seconds. So we made our way along one of the endless corridors that led to gate 34, and the Thomsonfly 737 to Tenerife, and as I write these notes, we are flying along the South Coast, over Cornwall and out over Lands End, turning sharp left at The Isles of Scilly, heading south for The Canaries. We could have got picked up! Not sure Lands End could have coped, but I bet Newquay could have.

Tuesday 20th November 2007, Penzance Station, 10pm.

Photo taken by my daughter, Rebecca. L-R, Jake, Paul, Baggins, Me, Chris, Dawn, Danielle

21st November 2007 (by Jen)

Well the latest update is that Paul and Steve left Cornwall yesterday to spend 11 days in La Gomera, doing the compulsory final boat checks, which are required by Woodvale. No doubt they will also enjoy the beaches, sunshine, swimming pools and a few beers now and again, just to be social of course.

More money was raised last weekend when more people entered the competition to guess how long the row would take. The winner will receive £50.

Unfortunately we don't yet know how much money has been raised for the local charity, Cornwall Hospice Care (formerly St.Julias Hospice and Mount Edgecumbe Hospice)as donations continue to be received, but we will of course let everyone know, when we do have a definite figure.

Paul and Steve will be sending back regular reports regarding their progress throughout the row and these will be published on the website "blog" for everyone to read.

STEVE AND PAUL KNOW THE REASON WHY

The Cornishman Newspaper Article – 22nd November 2007

As usual, there are several intrepid Cornish rowers taking on the challenge of rowing The Atlantic Ocean, and this time I expect the County to split in two, with West Cornwall supporting Steve Gardner and Paul Harris from Penzance on "The Reason Why" and East Cornwall supporting Nick Histon and John Csehi from Fowey on "Row4Cornwall".

There have been four Atlantic races to date, in 1997, 2001, 2003 and 2005, and The Cornish have been very well represented in the previous races. In 1997 I was delighted to follow the exploits of three of the 17 competitors, all with family connections here in The West Country. My good friend, St.Mawes based boatbuilder Jon Leach, built the entry"Golden Fleece" for Daniel Innes and Andrew Whittaker, which completed the crossing in 61 days. Unfortunately, due to injury, Andrew had to be replaced at very short notice by Pete Lowe, and it was highly creditable to start let alone finish, as Pete had not trained for 60 odd days at sea! Russell Reid with Andrew Watson rowed across in 64 days on board "Bitzer". Fowey boys Louis Hunkin and Michael Elliott, on board "Cornish Challenger" took 66 days, but had the satisfaction of both building and rowing their own boat. Indeed it was the exploits of Louis and Michael, that persuaded Nick, Michael's cousin, to embark on the same mad adventure. Two years ago Chris Barrett and Bob Warren from St.Mawes had a really good stab at the event, sadly capsizing, "Spirit of Cornwall" when almost in sight of Antigua.

Both crews have really worked hard to get to The Canaries with the initial challenge being to raise the finance to purchase the rowing boats, which are supplied in kit form. The "kits" (ply sheets with the pieces marked to be cut out and assembled), were dispatched by race organisers Woodvale Events in October last year, and the crews have worked through the Winter to both launch their completed craft in early Spring. Combining fitness training with boat building (as well as having full time jobs), is no easy task, and although just rowing The Atlantic is some achievement, ever since the first race back in 1997, it has been treated as a serious race.

In 1997, New Zealanders Rob Hamill and Phil Stubbs rowed from Tenerife to Barbados in 41 days, and set a standard, successive competitors have sought to match, if not better. Fellow Kiwi's James Fitzgerald and Kevin Biggar, finally bettered the time by 24 hours in 2003.

The Penzance challenge in this year's event is strong, with both Steve and Paul being members of Zennor Gig Club, and having participated in several long distance rows in gigs. The 2550 nautical miles is obviously substantially longer than any previous row attempted, but I am confident they will get to English Harbour. The pair are raising money for Cornwall Hospice Care, and you can follow their progress and donate to their charity on their website, www.the-reason-why.co.uk;

The Fowey duo, Nick and Jon, do not have the experience of Steve and Paul, but do have youth on their side. Obviously bettering the time set by Mike Elliott and Louis Hunkin, of 66 days, will be their first priority, but I think there will be a keen battle for bragging rights between the two crews. Again the pair are using the row as a focus to raise money for charity, Epilepsy and Cancer being the chosen charities and donations can be made on, www.row4cornwall.co.uk; I saw the row4cornwall team at the Southampton boat show, after Nick and Jon had rowed from Fowey as part of their training programme.

Indeed both crews have been rowing along the Cornish coast over the summer months so you may well have met one or the other of the Cornish Challengers during their preparation for next Sunday. Nothing to date will prepare them, however, for the daunting task that they will embark upon. The sore hands, the blisters on bums, the sunstroke and sheer mental and physical effort, you cannot help but wish both crews success. The human spirit is a precious and rare commodity, which can, if challenged, overcome all adversity and hardship. I can think of no bigger challenge than rowing The Atlantic and I hope our Cornish lads do themselves, and us proud.

The Reason Why (and others), in La Gomera...where you can clearly see the precision, purpose made cradles (sometimes known as pallets!) on which all the boats were shipped!!!

23rd November 2007

After landing in Tenerife, we caught a Monty Pythonesque licensed bandit in a taxi, who took us to the ferry port, without worrying about speed limits, lanes or other traffic, and I remember thinking that if the row is half as scary as the taxi ride....I'm not going!

We spent a few hours in Los Cristianos, the ferry port, waiting for the ferry, funnily enough. The very large, (three separate bars!) triple hulled Fred Olsen Tenerife to La Gomera ferry, trying a few beers in the sweltering heat, and having some memorable garlic prawns.

It was hot...really hot, and judging by the amount of bare brown flesh on show, it had been for some time. Everywhere seemed full of burnt people wearing ankle socks, three quarter trousers and England football shirts, the ones that had anything on at all that is! Although the giant Mount Teidy towered over us and did it's best to be the amazing sight it obviously is, with its summit lost in the clouds, (at 3718 metres, it is the highest mountain in all of Spain, let alone the Canaries!), I can't say that I found Tenerife very appealing, and I hoped La Gomera was a bit less touristy, and more to my liking.

We caught the ferry to La Gomera, eventually, after leaving the very pleasant bar and standing in the sun for an hour, before we realised that a certain person had his watch 1 hour too far on, as we were still on UK time here!

Los Cristianos, Tenerife and the Fred Olsen Ferry to La Gomera

I suppose I should tell you how horrible it is here in La Gomera, quiet as the grave, no bars, no restaurants, no shops and nothing to do but work, work, work on the boat, and it's cold, damp and nasty...problem is, it isn't. It is really nice, and if not quiet, it is hot, and has more bars and restaurants than you can shake a stick at!

San Sebastian – capital of La Gomera

The food so far has been superb, and the "solo mio", steak in a creamy pepper sauce, is our particular favourite. As with most places you visit, one bar in particular becomes your favourite, and here the dubious honour belongs to "The Blue Marlin" run by a splendid chap who answers to Manuel or Manola, whilst continually telling everyone that he is 51, and doesn't he look well for it! Being a very social chap, you find that if you include him in each round of drinks, as the evening wears on, the rounds get decidedly cheaper!

The bar is a Mecca for rowers and sailors either en route, or about to embark across The Atlantic. It also attracts a good compliment of locals who come to watch the "idiots", and soak up the great atmosphere, of what is effectively an old style English pub...no food or restaurant...just drinks! The place is full of memorabilia, with a particularly striking and busy ceiling, (very like to The Mermaid on Scilly!), which is covered with dangling antiquities, (and that is not a reference to Paul and me, by the way!). Every now and again, and there is no set pattern to it, Manuel will start all the things hanging from the ceiling swinging! This includes a hammock full of flags, old clothes, and teddy bears, alongside several large, very real, smoked pork hams! Very occasionally, when he gets to know you better, he may cut you a slice off and present it to you to eat...it is very strong tasting and very smoky, as they still smoke in the pubs over here! No one really knows the purpose, or why he does the swinging ritual, but it just is that sort of place....and you just have to be there!

Manuel (or Manola), behind the bar of his truly splendid "Blue Marlin"

We have had The Reason Why scrutinised by Simon and Tony from Woodvale, and apart from a missing Captains medical book, that we wouldn't use anyway, and a few minor suggestions that we don't really agree with, and will ignore, we are cleared to go!!!

The Woodvale boat park, and if you look closely, you may see Mr. Harris...

...and the moment Droops the Watch Pig was super glued to the aft cabin roof!

The part about working on the boat is true, well today it was, we spent all day either on it, or fetching 150 litres of water (our emergency supply and self righting ballast) from the supermarket. This involved wheeling 30no, 5 litre bottles of water in two supermarket trolleys, with their own idea on steering just like the English ones, right through the centre of the town, up and down kerbs and over cobbles. This attracted a bit of attention from the locals, at first bewilderment, and later amusement as all 23 boats did the same thing, making it a fairly common sight.

With regard to the missing medical book, we've decided that the one we have will do for us, and we have made a pact, that on no account would either of us perform some kind of half arsed surgery on the other...nor will we eat each other. We will pass together with our dignity intact if it comes to it!

We have bought a tin opener, sun cream, coffee, a bottle of port and a bottle of rum, which seemed sort of right somehow, even though neither of us are rum drinkers! (addendum...little did we know how important the rum was to become to us, particularly as we completely failed to take any chocolate, sweets or treats of any kind...what a pair of plonkers!!).

We should have our tracking beacon fitted tomorrow (the thing that will turn us into a dot!) then we can start packing everything away in its right place in the boat. The weather has been hot, but it does tend to cloud up early and late, and there is the threat of rain. I am sitting writing this report, wearing only a pair of shorts, as close to the open window of our hotel room as possible, just to try and get a bit of breeze, which is not at all cold, even though it is 7pm and dark. All the other crews seem very friendly, it's like one big family here, all getting ready for the same main event, but most of them seem to be busily working on their boats around the clock, as some appear to be only half finished! None of them seem to be as ready to go as ours, and some are in bits, with major fit outs still to do, water makers not fitted or tested, batteries not tested or charged , and in at least one case...not even purchased yet!

Bill and Peter, the South Africans, are great, and have hardly ever mentioned the rugby, in fact they have been very complimentary about England, who they said made the World Cup. For some reason I don't understand their boat, "Gquma Challenger" isn't here yet, and is stuck on Las Palmas, but should arrive tomorrow...they hope. One of the all girl pairs crew is Elin and Herdip, their boat "Dream Maker" still needs a bit of work, and it was them that were at Newark in front of us, whose boat we turned around...twice! Elin plays ladies rugby for Wales, and as Wales play South Africa in a day or two, we were going to find a bar to watch it, should be a bit of fun.

The girls in "Unfinished Business" are on one side of us, still fitting hatches and painting constantly. Scott and Neil in "Ocean Summit" are the other side, with not that much left to do. The Irish lads in "C2", and the Frenchmen in "Pygram" are not here yet, and nor are the four policemen from the Met. in "Mission Atlantic". Simon Chalk's "Oyster Shack" is right behind us, but is barely more than a shell, and surely won't be ready for his record attempt with the rest of us?

We obviously got it wrong, and should have left a lot more work to do on the boat once we got here...but we didn't....damn it, just have to go to the pub again!

Jon and Nick, the two Cornish lads in their boat "No Fear" are the other side of the road, working away feverishly on the boat, and they are next to a couple of Royal Marine Commando's, Ben and Orlando in "Go Commando", which apparently is none other than the all conquering "All Relative" that won the 2005 race by a couple of weeks. This is a fours class boat and carbon fibre composite construction, none of your plywood there. Not sure how that qualifies for the pairs race? Orlando, as his name may suggest, is quite a bit in your face and full of how far they are going to win by! We'll see what happens as we plod along behind, our priority has always been to get there first and race second.

"Pura Vida" is a fours boat right at the end of the quay, seemingly in bits, but we like Carl, Robbie, John and Tom a lot, and I think it just looks worse than it is, with a mountain of food and kit spread all over the quay. "Moveahead 2" is next to them, another fours boat, but actually, this one makes "Pura Vida" look finished. One of the chaps from "Moveahead 2" was moaning about Expedition foods (we got a lot of stuff from them as well), "...sends us a bill for £2500, gives us a measly 10% discount and then presents us with his sticker longer than the F...ing boat!" I don't think that sticker ever made it on to his boat.

"Atlantic Jack" and "Spirit of Fernie" are also over the other side, but whenever we go for a wander over there, there is never anyone at the boats, so we have not spoken to either of them yet. Back over in the Woodvale pen, the "Jaydoubleyou" brothers were coming along quietly, looking young and fit, and not shouting about how good they are, unlike some of the others, they may be dark horses if they can row. James and especially Niall in "Komale" are extremely bullish about how quick their boat is, and are not shy in saying that they think they have a great chance of winning. We are always bumping into Pete, a solo Australian rower in "Charmed Life" with it seems a great deal of work still to do on the boat, but his parents and girlfriend are helping him full time.

The young girls, or "Atlantic Angels" as they call themselves, one of whom is only 17, have no shortage of offers to help with their boat, "Silver Cloud" for some reason! There is always someone working on it. We see Rachel and Lin every morning at breakfast, as they are in the same hotel as us, "The Garonjay." They seem very well organised and sponsored to the hilt, with their boat "Barbara Ivy". Angela and Franck are an unlikely couple in "Bout de Vie", as Angela is a very accomplished disabled rower in a wheelchair, and Franck has only one leg. They are amazing people to even attempt this, and we have nothing but admiration for them. Also, as Angela is American and doesn't speak French, and Franck is French and doesn't speak much English, should be an interesting if quiet crossing, good luck to them. Their boat is probably the furthest behind, and it will be touch and go to be ready in time.

The boys in "Pendovey Swift" we haven't spoken to yet, and neither have we to the chaps in "Titanic Challenge", but as Paul said, and I agree with him. "I wouldn't go to sea in a boat with that name tag, not if you paid me!"

All of Paul's many superstitions must be rubbing off on me, never take a pasty in a boat, nor three cornered sandwiches, green boats are bad (how we get him in our green gigs is beyond me!), albatross's are a common one, and ....I'll have to whisper this ...rabbits! You mustn't even mention the "r" word in or even near a boat! In Padstow, they are so superstitious about this, that they no longer call them rabbits, they have renamed them " fur liners", just in case.

Anyway, that's us all caught up, we will send more news soon for Jen to publish. A big thank you to everyone for their best wishes, and love to our families. I can hear the Blue Marlin calling, and some food besides Pringles seems like a good idea!

It is a funny thing, but now we are here, in La Gomera, it feels like a great many of the obstacles stacked against us in getting this great adventure to a successful end, have been removed. Paul and I both feel it, looking out across the Ocean, it seems as if Antigua is just over the horizon, and there is nothing else in our way now. Not money, not equipment or stores, nothing. All we have to do is to row from here to there!

24th November 2007

Amanda came and sealed our 30no. 5 litre water bottle tops,(we get penalised in the race if we have used more than 50 litres, or if we had used some and not replaced it with sea water, to keep the weight and ballast the same). We stowed the water away in the below deck compartments of the boat, along the keel, carefully lining each compartment with bubble wrap first, and they fitted so snugly, that they could have been made to measure. We then packed in the bags of food and more bubble wrap to fill the voids, so if we were to capsize, the ballast water would stay against the keel, in the best place to assist the self righting. After a couple of hours of packing away the mountains of food, (and it was mandatory to take enough food for us both for 90 days, even though we were more than hopeful we wouldn't be anywhere near as long as that), amazingly, I thought, it is all going to fit.....how the hell we are going to eat it all... is another matter!

25th November 2007

We had a lazy day today, sitting on the boat in the sun, recovering from last night when some absolute bounder spiked our tonic water with gin! We have taken a lot of photos, but I have managed to forget my camera lead, so it will only be Paul's photos we send until we get back. After sending the last report, there was a sort of impromptu fancy dress party, but judging by some of the costumes, it wasn't that impromptu, but as our scrutineering didn't finish until after nine, we just went as a couple of dirty, unshaven ne'er do wells...normal night in the Blue Marlin really! The new official race website was launched yesterday, www.atlanticrowingrace2007.co.uk; (if you look at it quickly, it looks like, "at last I crow in grace"...or is it me?). We have some more photos of boats and "The Reason Why" being launched into the marina.

Had a massive paella for two on Friday, it had mussels and prawns as big as your head...well nearly. It has been a bit rainy lately and the wind keeps blowing, funnelling down the streets of the town, and there are often white tops on the sea, away from the shelter of the island. We both hope the wind keeps going our way for Sunday, to give us a quick start! We had a welcome meeting, they gave us a t-shirt and times of various other meetings we have to attend through the week, and the last thing will be the race of ocean boats, which is the La Gomera Cup, on Friday or Saturday. This was started 2 years ago when the start of the main race was delayed. Hopefully it won't be delayed this time, but the La Gomera Cup appears to be a regular fixture now, whatever. Actually, Stu, the captain of one of the support yachts, "Sara", told us that the Azores high is in position earlier than usual this year, which is apparently good, and should help to stabilise the normal weather patterns for this part of the Atlantic.

They managed to drop the rear end of T.R.Y. on her keel, but she seems ok!

We had the boat fully packed by Saturday lunchtime, and Neil and Scott of "Ocean Summit" next to us, were also ready, so Amanda from Woodvale organized both boats to be lifted into the water. This was done by 5pm ish, so we are now tied up, afloat, in the marina, once again next to "Ocean Summit".

The Reason Why and Ocean Summit

La Gomera marina

Neil from Ocean Summit having a crafty look at T.R.Y.

We were invited to a G&T party on "Sara" the support yacht by Stu and Andrea, which was great fun, and very generous of them, but as they ran out of tonic before they ran out of gin, you can understand why we are having a lazy day! Also seem to have made a pact with the "Pura Vida" boys last night, to wear their wristbands and not take them off, until we successfully reach Antigua and complete the race!

The marina teems with life, fish of every colour and size, but although there is a poster, I couldn't tell you which fish is which...especially as it's in Spanish!

We also had the good fortune to meet Guy, the mad Fin, his yacht is moored next to us (the one behind Neil in the photo). He is so larger than life, and just what I needed this morning in my fragile state, at least he didn't ask how long it was going to take or where are you going from. But when he presented us with a very smelly, Finnish garlic sausage, then stripped off and dived into the marina, nearly sinking the pontoon, it all became too much , and we resolved to go for a wander.

26th November 2007

Well, more time has been spent in the Blue Marlin, and there has been a lot more ham swinging! Had a Chinese last night, completely cocked up the order, and managed to get double of everything...we were stuffed. We daren't send it back as we took so long over trying to get it right...and failed. We laughed later.

Bad news from Chris at home, Baggins our dog has had a stroke. He's sort of ok, but it's a bit upsetting, especially with me being away.

We've been packing more stuff away on the boat, and bubble wrapped everything in tightly. The wind is still up, everyone thinks it could be a quick crossing, we'll see. Guy, our friendly Fin, was on song again today, in between eating lunch, drinking wine and suddenly leaping in the marina, nearly sinking us every time! I have to repeat how alive with marine life it is (not counting Guy!), bright blue fish with flowing tails, some like angel fish, John Dory, Mullett and long thin Barracuda like things that scatter the little ones. Last night we saw an octopus, just swimming along the surface, then it clung on to a mooring buoy, then off it went again - unbelievable.

I must stress to you all, we are NOT on holiday here, the fact that we have been sipping iced coke and eating toasted ham, egg, cheese and tomato sandwiches (it's their special), under gently swaying palms, until we retired to the beach in our shorts, actually it's too hot and we may have get back under the palms soon I'm starting to burn, is merely an illusion. We have to be here...we don't like it, but there it is.

Will sort some names and boats as we have to thank a few of them for their help, here are a few pictures of some of them, more soon, love to all Steve and Paul.

| **Barbara Ivy** | **Charmed Life** | **No Fear** | **Ocean Summit** |

Silver Cloud   **Go Commando**   **Row of Life**   **Gquma Challenge**

28th November 2007

Firstly, must thank Pete in "Charmed Life" for the rope, and Ian and Andy in "C2" for the loan of the fenders- we have now bought our own, but it is one big family here and everyone mucks in to help whoever needs it. Manuel was in fine ham swinging form the other night, and gave out some promotional bits and bobs...Paul got a bag of some sort but I got a T-shirt, which was very handy, as most of mine can walk to the pub on their own now!

We took the boat out yesterday and did ok against the wind. We went out again today, and the wind has dropped, and it seems like conditions are perfect. We had Antigua right on course with the GPS, today, and it was all I could do to stop Paul setting off now! A gently following 1 knot breeze, allowed us to put our feet up while testing the water maker, which performed perfectly, by the way. It was then we decided to go fishing, and test out our sophisticated fishing equipment ... two £1.99 hand lines from Lidl's... much to the amusement of a passing Woodvale support yacht. Of course, I did all the donkey work, dangling the lures etc. handed it to Paul who almost immediately pulled up a great spiny looking fish! Don't worry Chris...we threw it back.

Compasses and GPS's all seem coordinated now, so our deviation is just the standard 7 degrees that the book tells us. Well that's the technical bit done, I feel a bit like Arthur Dent most of the time, and just say "I don't understand" and "Where's the tea?" We got well set up for today on the usual feast of cheese and ham breakfast, still the first items on the menu of international cuisine. We are now back ashore on this fair isle, and may have to go for lunch soon...may have cheese and ham!

Good news from home, for those who don't know, Baggins is recovering well from his stroke, he's not out of the woods yet, but Chris says he's much better.

We ate at "El Pajar" last night, a great little place that is sort of inside out, with palm trees growing up between tables and a gutter that runs around the inside of a pantile roof with the middle open to the sky. The place seems to be alive with raffeta panels sort of growing up the walls and across the ceiling. The food was great, a "solo mio" creamy pepper steak, we have a lot of those. The locals sat in the corner watching Seville beat Arsenal 2-1.

We gave Manuel a t-shirt, which he put on, and a sticker, which he put on the front wine fridge in pride of place, and celebrated with a special ham swinging.

A big hello to Wombwell Homes, hope all ok without me, hope you haven't rented out my desk! We (mainly Paul of course) have been impressing the "Pura Vida" boys, by splicing some ropes together for them, and helping anybody who needs it, as we are ready to go!

Right, our crisis ops meeting beckons, will send more news soon...love to all Steve and Paul.

T.R.Y. in all her glory, photo by Lin and Rachel from Barbara Ivy

A quiet night in the Blue Marlin!   "El Pajar"

It is at this point, that I have to say, that if the scurrilous and malicious rumour surfaces, that a certain Cornish Gig Rower, took a wrong turn to the toilet the other night, went out of his room by mistake and found himself standing in the brightly lit hotel entrance in his under pants, looking lost and not a little dazed (not as dazed as the night porter peering round the door of his office at a nearly naked man in his lobby), who then woke up everyone in the hotel except the other Cornish Gig Rower who remained completely zonked behind the self locking door of their shared room. Eventually he let him back in, but needless to say the entire episode will be vigourously denied as a complete fabrication!

29th November 2007

More cheese and ham for breakfast, but with fresh peaches and pineapple this time, after which, Woodvale organized a coach trip to the other side of the island for anyone who had their boats ready and were just killing time awaiting the start. I am glad we went, as the island of La Gomera is amazing. Along with Juan the coach driver and Petra, our Spanish and English speaking German guide, we left the hot and dry San Sebastian in the south, and went off into the very different, lush, wet and mountainous north. Giant rock monoliths tower thousands of feet over massive tiered valleys, where farmers have cultivated their crops over the millennia. There are trees full of dates, figs, lemons, oranges, avocados and bananas, lining the twisting, winding roads that loop up thousands of feet only to come back down again in true Italian Job style hair pins.

Great palm trees sway in the gentle breeze, as Petra, in her own distinctive, multi-lingual way, and in almost perfect English...unfortunately minus the letters R and V...describes the "winyards", "twees", the lush "wegitation", (and the one that finished us off), before we get to the "wisitor centre". Sad really but we had a fit of uncontrollable school boy giggles, which we couldn't stop...twagic really!!!

The complimentary three course traditional La Gomeran meal and free wine was superb, but so filling we could barely move for the afternoon, but full marks to Woodvale for organizing it, we thoroughly enjoyed ourselves.

North La Gomera   "La Fortaleza"   Lion rock   Northern Valleys

We have just had a course meeting, and have plotted our proposed course on the chart, but basically we will go with the wind, as long as it is generally in our favour. There are rumours of a weather front coming our way, which would be typical, after the weather being perfect while we sat here for 10 days. Apparently the front, if it arrives, isn't enough to put back the start...apparently! We have also unanimously voted to let "Komale" start a day or two after everyone else, as Niall has somehow managed to get a poisoned arm and the doctor won't let him go yet.

Tomorrow is the La Gomera Cup, which is likely to be more of a procession than a race, as it was, at its inaugural running two years ago. We have a chap called Hilary, from The Cornish Independent coming to meet us tomorrow, and he wants to do an interview and take some photos. Richard, thanks for the lovely Engine House pic???

Thanks for all the messages of support. We heard that a friend of Paul's, has won a competition to name a new Skinners beer...it will be called "Manacle". I think this name suits a spirit more than a pint, then you could have a Manacle on the rocks!

30th November 2007

Just a note to say that we spent last night in The Blue Marlin with Joss and Ian of "Pendovey Swift", and had a great laugh with them. Apparently Ian has won The London River Race, which Paul and I have taken part in several times, in gigs. Joss, who is ultra competitive, has never won it, despite several attempts to do so. This fact doesn't irritate or annoy him at all...well not much, only while he's awake! Once we realised this, of course we didn't keep mentioning it every 5 minutes all night, because that would wind him up. Joss assured us later that the smoke coming out of his ears, had more to do with the beer and it being a hot night, than the fact that Ian has apparently won The London River Race...or have I mentioned that?

If you ever read this Joss, sorry... but it was funny.

1st December 2007

Hello folks, here it is, the very last entry of our "Pre-Race Blog", from your "definitely not on holiday but preparing for the row" correspondent in sunny and hot La Gomera. Jen will be publishing all future entries in the "Race Blog" on the website. We met Hilary who did an interview and took photos, should be in Sunday Independent on 9th December. This afternoon, while Paul was learning all the necessaries of the satellite phone, I went to make an Antiguan flag, as it is a courtesy to fly the flag of the country whose waters you enter, from abroad. Do you know, the Chinese Bazaar here, has everything. I thought they might have pens in the right colours, but permanent felt tip pens especially for writing and colouring cloth, was beyond my wildest hopes. So I "borrowed" an old threadbare pillowcase from the hotel linen cupboard, downloaded a copy of the Antiguan flag from the internet, and drew up and coloured in, a double sided flag of Antigua. It wasn't bad either. Couldn't get one here, and Paul refused to pay the £34 they cost at home!

Last night we went to the Woodvale farewell barbeque, at which the race start WAS confirmed as planned for tomorrow at 12 noon. We managed (all 23 crews not just us!) to eat the barbequed fish and drink the three barrels of free beer, but not before catching a glimpse of the very rare La Gomeran Nocturnal Albino Bag Lizard, high on the cliff above us. I managed to get a very blurred and unclear photo, and it caused quite a stir with everyone trying to get a glimpse of the 2 foot white monster.

BBQ, beer, beard and Pura Vida wristbands ... and the mighty Albino Bag Lizard!

The party continued in The Blue Marlin later, and although it was more of a procession or parade this morning, for The La Gomera Cup, as the cup was donated by Manuel, Simon Chalk stood up to award it anyway. After a discussion between Simon, Manuel and the other Woodvale people there, Simon announced, "For being the most laid back crew on and off the water, which includes going fishing and catching one, for being the most organized and prepared crew, and the crew that has done more to boost the coffers of the "Manuel retirement fund" than anyone else....it must go to ... "The Reason Why!!!" Well, talk about proud and shocked. The bar erupted, and we, me that is, had to say a thank you speech on a stool...you should see the cup, well you will, as we are bringing it home, and have to bring it back in 2 years for the start of the 2009 race.

There were various other memorable moments, that frankly, I can't remember, but most revolved around the Blue Marlin...including Manuel in a policeman's helmet trying to arrest the four coppers from the Met. in "Mission Atlantic", the fancy dress night, and again, Manuel trying to get the same four policemen to keep the noise down when they were determined to start singing one night, long after midnight. Elin's rugby tackle that cleared out everyone, including tables. But the final memory is of Robbie, from "Pura Vida" diving off the bar into the crowd below, after dropping his trousers and setting light to his pubic hair! It was crazy, and I still can't get the smell of burning hair out of my nose. There are no pictures of that, thank goodness, but the few photos I do have of the last night, follow..

We have just stocked the boat up with fresh fruit, and practiced the sat phone options, Paul has it sussed, I've got my Arthur Dent head on again when it comes to technical stuff! It is quite strange to see the clock on the website without days on it, just hours. I will be glad to see it counting up again as we get going!

It is getting close now, stocking up on cheese and ham, as Chris Jenkins of "the Scilly Boys" just turned up to see the start and took us for lunch, and we wish him and his crew the best of luck for their attempt on the North Atlantic next year.

This is the last blog before we go, and I'll leave you with what Simon Chalk has just announced, "Everything appears in place for a very fast crossing and records will be broken!" We'll wait and see, but it sounds promising.

That's it! The time has come the walrus said to talk of many things, of ships and shoes and sealing wax, and cabbages and kings, and why the sea is boiling hot and whether pigs have wings....well pretty soon, we may be able to tell you, as Paul, Droops the Watch Pig complete with binder twine lead, and myself, make our merry way across The Atlantic Ocean. Thank you for all the support and messages, love to family and friends, see you all soon.   Steve and Paul xx

Strange But True...

One of the strangest stories we were told whilst in La Gomera, concerns the boat "Moveahead" from the 2005 race, which was a pairs boat crewed by Bobby Prentice and Colin Briggs.

Unfortunately, on day 49 of the race, three days after the capsize of "Team Sun Latte" and "American Fire", "Moveahead" suffered the same fate, of capsize and rescue, however, it is the rescue of Bobby and Colin that is the strangest story...

With their boat upturned and life raft deployed, both men were being thrown all over the place by a rough sea, for several hours, as they waited for someone to respond to their E.P.I.R.B. (Emergency Position Indicating Radio Beacon) distress signal. Eventually they spotted a large yacht heading towards them, and after some tricky manoeuvring in the lumpy sea, it came alongside, and despite Bobby and Colin, understandably, not being at their best, they were successfully taken on board the yacht, and ...rescued, or at least so it appeared.

Bearing in mind the two rowers were badly shaken, sick, cold, wet and tired, mentally and physically, it was still apparently fairly obvious straight away to them, that there was something odd about the yacht. Safe on deck, the bewildered and totally exhausted Bobby and Colin, were not allowed to go anywhere else! They were made to stay up on deck, and it was made clear to them that below decks was out of bounds completely. There was no explanation, and very little talk at all, until after a while, a large tanker "Potomac" appeared over the horizon, apparently also in response to the distress signal from "Moveahead".

As the large vessel got nearer, amazingly, Bobby and Colin were forced to jump back into the uninviting and far from calm sea they had just been pulled out of, and return to the life raft!! This they struggled back into, after the shortest "rescue" on record, and were cast adrift once more, as the yacht they had been so pleased to see, sailed off and left them, presumably assuming they would be rescued for a second time, by the fast approaching "Potomac".

I don't know what if any radio communications took place between yacht and tanker, if any, but obviously the yacht didn't want to be involved, and was certainly "up to something"...presumably no good! Strange that the yacht had bothered in the first place, showing enough compassion and humanity in obeying maritime etiquette and responding to the distress call as nearest vessel, but then having no compunction in washing their hands of all responsibility, passing the "rescue" on to another vessel at the first opportunity, presumably to maintain their anonymity.

"Potomac" did safely rescue Bobby and Colin, for a second time, but after an experience like that, it is once again amazing to see them both out here once more, teaming up with Billy Blunden and Ted Manning, to make up a fours crew, to try again in " Moveahead 2". Once again their courage and resolve must demand our utmost respect, and we give it unreservedly, and wish them the best of luck.

"My Arse!" muttered Paul, in a very Jim Royal like manner, for the forty-second time today.

I lay back in the cabin, hatch open, and reached for the Sat. Phone, there were nine new text messages. Several hello's and best wishes, four from Jennie giving our position, our daily mileage, where everybody else was, the weather forecast, and any other assorted news She thought we should know. There was the fifth message of the day from Andrew Turner, demanding that we row like warriors and overtake "those bloody Springboks!" Then there was the daily quote guessing game from Sam, my eldest.

Some of the quotes I got, some I didn't, but I had grown to look forward to this little game each day, which she kept up for the entire trip. "If anyone sees me go near a boat again, they have my permission to shoot me!" was a more obvious one, while "Youth cannot know how age thinks and feels, but old men are guilty if they forget what it was to be young...and I seem to have forgotten lately!" was more obscure.

"My Arse!" I exclaimed out loud, easing down my rowing shorts and reaching for the life savers, baby wipes and "sudocream", my rowing stint over for an hour.

The "Sea-Me" radar suddenly bleeped into life, making me jump, and indicating that we were not alone. "Keep your eyes open, we've got company" I called to Paul out on the oars. I noticed the AIS radar had been switched off (it would bleep sometimes for no reason we could see, and keep us awake), so I switched it back on and it too, immediately bleeped at me, confirming we were in for a visit from someone.

I turned to the radar screen, and there She was, coming from the North-East, a container ship called "Cala Pura". This would be the ninth tanker we had encountered, and like some of the others, it was travelling at 16.8 knots, and this was the important bit, it was coming straight at us!

"Any sign, Paul, this one looks close" I called to Paul, "Can't see a thing, nothing but sea" he replied. "It's still 6.8 nautical miles away, but it is shifting, and the track line shows it's coming straight at us." "Hang on...I can see her" called Paul

I climbed out of the cabin, and stood up to look where Paul was pointing, and as we rose on the swell, sure enough, there she was.Paul stopped rowing as we tried to work out which side of us she would pass, and how best to take avoiding action. After a few minutes, we could see that if we stopped rowing, it would pass across our bow, as long as she didn't change course that is. "Call her up" said Paul

So I reached for the hand held VHF radio, and switched it on, "This is ocean rowing boat "The Reason Why" calling tanker "Cala Pura" over...." nothing. So I called again, and this time a fairly surprised sounding voice burst out from the radio speaker in my hand, making me nearly drop it... "Hello, who is calling "Cala Pura?" said a voice in broken English.

"This is ocean rowing boat "The Reason Why" en route from La Gomera to Antigua, saw you were close on the radar, and thought we'd give you call to make sure you'd seen us...over"

"No!" came back the reply, and then, "Rowing, are you in trouble...do you need assistance? What is your exact position and how big are you?...Antigua??...speak slow so I can understand please...over"

"No, no trouble, we don't need anything thanks, just letting you know we're here. We are17degrees 02.66minutes North, 54 degrees 22.29 minutes West, and we are small, a 23 foot rowing boat...over"

"You speak too quick, wait I have you on radar, we will pass North, no problem, you sure you're not in trouble, do you need anything?" "No Thanks we're fine" I replied. "I give weather forecast, Antigua, very big wind in Caribbean, 25-30 knots, big sea too, but good for you, wind is East...going your way...and sunshine, then dropping 15-20 knots later ... you want nothing then?"

"No, nothing thanks, but thanks for the weather forecast, sounds good, over and out"

He never replied, but we sat and watched the great ship go past, loaded up with containers, across our bow, about 250-300 yards away to the North of us, and disappear to the South-West.

As I lay back in the cabin, another text came in, the one I was hoping for, from my daughter Sam. Not a quote this time, but a short and very important message that read, "You can now call me Doctor Gardner!" love Sam

Sam had got her PhD, and I had a very proud moment, as a tear tried to escape down my cheek, as I attacked a celebratory box of Pringles.

"My Arse!" said Paul, settling back down to rowing again...excitement over.

(Incidentally, I'm glad we didn't rely on the "CalaPura" weather forecast, as it was completely useless, and for the next three days we were beset with continual squalls and heavy rain. No sunshine, and the wind was a difficult North East, not East, and between squalls, it was light not strong....apart from that, he was right on!)

CHAPTER 6 – FINALLY...THE START!!

Prayer to Mo

Mighty ocean hear our prayer

And grant us leave your world to share

That we may see your majesty

And gaze upon your beauty free

There'll be no victory or defeat

If you allow our worlds to meet

And let us safely be as one

Together till our journey done

Mighty ocean you're the boss

Please grant our wish and let us cross.

sg 2007

Well, that's it, all the waiting around and endless preparations are over, and it's finally time to go. We were called to a 9am. photo call, which in true Woodvale tradition, took place at 10am. Farewell handshakes and goodbye hugs, then we were out on the water, milling around the start line, and the support yachts, "Sara" and "Kilcudden", "Sara" acting as start boat as well.

We emptied our pockets of all coinage, and threw it overboard, in an offering to Neptune for a safe passage, this was Paul's idea...and a good one, as we'll take all the help we can get, mental as well as physical, and being on good terms with the ocean was important.

I had prepared a short prayer for just this moment, and with Paul's approval, it was now that I said it. (Why I neglected to put it in the original blog at this point I have no idea, actually it was only called "Prayer to Mo" later on).

The five minute warning sounded, and then the countdown to the off at 12 noon began. It was a beautiful hot sunny day and the sea was calm, as Stu on board "Sara" counted down from 10..........

We had a good start, but Joss and Ian in Pendovey Swift shot off, had I mentioned that Ian had won The London River Race...poor Joss. The South African's, Pete and Bill, got away well too, with Nick and Jon in No Fear, Orlando and Ben in Go Commando and Scott and Neil in Ocean Summit not far away. Pete and Bill had a problem with their auto helm later, and had to stop, but we never found out what it was. We went along the coast of La Gomera, at first and then started to turn south, and we wanted to stay well clear of the small island of El Hierro. After 17 miles, on day 1, La Gomera lay behind us and El Hierro lay in front, and the first night beckons.

They say the first night at sea on your own is hell...well it was...it wasn't good anyway. An Easterly cross wind blew up which tried to blow everyone on to El Hierro, before which we seemed to be in second place for a while, which surprised us. It was a big, choppy and messy sea, that led us into our first night of being thrown all over the place, and frankly, feeling sick. At first I daren't tell Paul that I was feeling sick, and apparently he was the same and didn't want to tell me. Once we realised this, we just settled to the fact, as Paul so eloquently put it, that we were "as sick as shags!"

Monday didn't get much better, as we were still feeling sick, and we had to cope with a constant choppy, cross sea, but we did have a chat, and took a vote NOT to have our low point in the trip just yet!

We saw our first wildlife, which was a dolphin on Monday evening, but the Easterly wind and choppy sea makes it very difficult, and we still can't eat anything and keep it down. The wind came and went, but it was never easy, and it kept it up all day into the second uncomfortable night, surfing waves in the dark we could not see!

Ready to go!   "Moveahead 2"   Simon Chalk final check

Sunday 2nd December the morning of the Start

Off at last, with Mount Teidy poking his nose above the Tenerife clouds, looking on

The line up for the start, the rocky coastline of La Gomera behind us

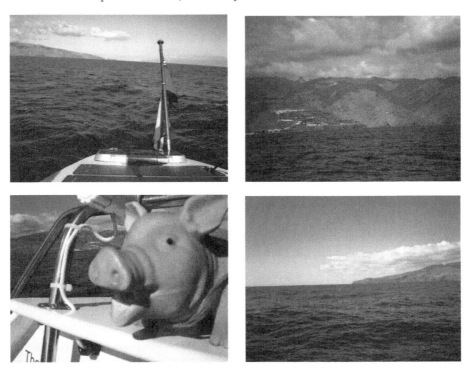

La Gomera was behind us, El Hierro and 3000 miles of Atlantic lay in front

Monday 3rd December 2007 (by Jen)

I have received some text messages and apparently the first night on the water was rough! "The Reason Why," and no doubt all the other boats were caught up in an Easterly Gale, which has caused seasickness to both Paul and Steve. Despite trying to continue rowing through big seas and gale force winds, they were forced to give up at 2am. They retreated to the cabin where they were thrown about for the rest of the night. However, they are both fine, and still in good spirits.

Rowing recommenced at 9am.this morning, and today has seen the boat coping well among the 25 foot waves. There has been a 3 knot wind blowing them in the right direction, and only one wave went over the stern of the boat, where the sleeping cabin is located, but unfortunately, this was at the very moment Paul opened the roof hatch! Accordingly, some of Steve's bedding is now rather wet. The seasickness is being kept at bay as long as they are rowing or lying down, try to stand or sit and watch out!

Apparently the island of El Hierro is very much like Paul Church, however much you row, you just can't get past it! Ask any Ladies "A" rower, and she'll know what you mean.

Most of the other boats have dispersed and are all out of sight now, but there were two meetings in the night, first when the boys looked out, after hearing shouts it was the other Cornish boat "No Fear", and later "Go Commando". "What are you doing?" called Orlando, "We're having a kip!" I shouted, "Clear off!" I can still hear him laughing.

Tuesday 4th December 2007

The second night was equally awful, and we were still poorly, however, in the morning we did manage to force some food down, the fresh oranges, apples and cherries were the best and when they actually stayed down, we opened a box of Pringles. We forced ourselves to row despite the sea/weather and the sun came up lovely, and for the first time, we realised that we were out of sight of land. We made an executive decision, and threw our plan out of the window. We turned the boat to go with the wind and sea, and at one point, we were making good time, and the GPS said we were heading straight for Antigua, ok, so it's still 2831 miles away, but as we head towards our first 100 miles at sea, we are starting to feel better. Had porridge and rice pudding, more cherries and a cup of tea, and hopefully we are past the initial sickness stage.

The waves have eased, but it is still a sloppy sea, but it is beautiful, Paul just spotted wildlife, a sea turtle, and another dolphin just before dark. Rowing much better now with the Easterly wind.

The third night was still sloppy, so we both rested, as we tied the rudder off, and let the wind take us in the right direction, at 1.7 – 2.2 knots.

We breakfasted on bangers and beans, and have also been snacking, and have copied previous rowers in giving the Atlantic a nickname, after the first line of our setting off prayer, She will be called "MO" (Mighty Ocean), but so far She's been "sloppy Mo!"

The sea continues to be all over the place at the moment, and Paul is trying to row, while I am propped up inside the cabin, trying to write this blog. It's like trying to type in a washing machine that's been turned on!

We will send more reports, or "blogs" as and when Mo settles down. Thank you all for the texts etc. we are receiving them, but won't be replying, as it is just too difficult at present. Love and best wishes to all friends and families, from us both.

Wednesday 5th December 2007

Position: 26' 40.50" N; 19'15.50" W; 1040 05/12/07

Overcast, sea still sloppy Mo.

Listened to Urban Hymns, Nirvana and Green Day. Note, Jake, your Dad likes Green Day live "Bullet in a Bible" so don't let him tell you otherwise. He doesn't, however, like Nirvana... "Bloody head banging music" is what he calls it...old git!!

I-Pod waterproof dock is brilliant...well spotted Rebecca.

Thursday 6th December 2007

The Weather is still disappointing, it is still very windy with overcast skies and big seas. I have composed a little poem, which about sums up the sea condition:

> We're surfing waves as big as houses
>
> That keep rolling through the night
>
> I keep looking for Antigua
>
> But the buggers' out of sight.
>
>
> In the day they're not much smaller
>
> But you see them as they pass
>
> As they fizzle right beside you
>
> And sometimes hit you up the arse.

Mo is still being very moody, but we are not downhearted. We are eating well and getting into a routine now. We both rather enjoy our baby wipe bed baths, glad we brought them. They really freshen you up when water is at a premium. We had enormous seas in the night, and we tried to set the drogues, but they wouldn't keep us straight, so we had to put out the sea anchor, and spent an awful night bouncing up and down, being pounded by waves!

Sun's just come up, I'm getting out of this cabin...it's hotter than hell!

Position: 26' 05.525" N; 20' 08.214" W. 1128, 06/12/07

Friday 7th December 2007

Today we were out early, and the weather got hot very quickly. We pulled up the sea anchor (which was easier said than done, full story will have to wait), and started making good ground again. The waves are generally 20 – 25 feet, and as I told Jen on the phone, we surfed one wave and recorded 7.8 knots. Fortunately all our seasickness has gone now, and it is amazing what we can do whilst bouncing up and down on the waves all the time.

We had a flying visitor in the night – "Pete the Petrel" who made a spectacular crash landing, bouncing off the cabin roof, then the deck and then hitting the water tank. He sat looking at me in amazement, and stayed for about 2 hours before flapping and flying off again.

(by Jen)

I have just received a telephone call from Steve. Good news, seasickness gone, but last night was another rough one, waves hitting them from every direction, including broadside on. They decided to deploy the para-anchor, but they were being bounced up and down so bad, they eventually went to check things out, and found the buoy had gone from the para-anchor, and so it had sunk 60 metres under the front of the boat, and this had caused the very rocky night in the cabin, and the exceptional bouncing effect on the bow. They managed to get the anchor up, and are rowing well again now. Today the ocean is "bad tempered Mo", with waves rising to at least 20 feet and some breaking over the boat. They appear to be averaging a good 3.5 knots, although while on the phone with Steve, the boat reached 7.8 knots on a wave, which Paul claimed as the fastest speed so far, obviously a bit of competition going on between them.

They have now been updated with their positions compared to all the other boats, and they are very happy with how things are going. Although only a mile from "No Fear", the chance of seeing them is very slim, as the horizon is only as far as the next wave. They are receiving messages of support from friends and family, but it is still too difficult to type or reply due to the rough conditions. They ask that I pass on thanks to everyone, and confirm they are absolutely fine and everything is going well.

From my Notebook/log; Mo consistently unpredictable! Now sickness gone, all day breakfast a winner! Have fun at the Gig Club/Pz Sailing Club dinner and dance tonight. Sorry for lack of dispatches, too bouncy! Sat. Phone playing up a bit too.

Position: 25' 47.657" N, 20' 47.886" W. 1219.07/12/07.

We received this e-mail from my daughter Sam: Hi Dad and Paul, you guys are doing great. It's amazing how many people are monitoring your progress, the website has had over 5000 hits so far, and rising all the time. I feel I want to do something to take your mind (if only slightly) off the sea (or sloppy Mo!). So, I will send you a quote every day, followed by the answer the next day, with the next quote, via the Iridium text on the satellite phone. If it gets annoying, just tell me to stop. Here's the first one (it should be obvious to you, Dad)...

"Human beings, who are almost unique in having the ability to learn from the experience of others, are also remarkable for their apparent disinclination to do so." Answer tomorrow, lots of love Sam

Thanks Sam, all good here, sunset lovely just now. Speak soon love Dad x.

(I will put the answers all together at the end of the book, so everyone can have a go)

Saturday 8th December 2007

Last night we had a good night and rowed right through the night. We did shifts of 1 hour on and 1 hour off till midnight, followed by 2 hours on and 2 hours off till 8 am, and we appear to have done some good mileage The wind has dropped a little, but the sea is still choppy, and it is hard to put 2 strokes together. Our knees are black and blue by being constantly hit by the oars, and we have blisters on various fingers and toes, all well plastered up, but nothing too serious. We are both well and still laughing!

We set waypoints at the start of the race, leg 1 took us to El Hierro, and leg 2 took us almost to where we are now. In about 40 miles we have to turn right at " Little Mo's roundabout at the centre of the universe" and start leg 3, which is only about 1300 miles long, if Mo lets us that is!

A few thanks, for all the texts and messages of support, especially to our support person Jen, our families, Chris, Sam, Bex, Ogz, Alex, Dawn, Jake and Danielle, Simon at Hot Dog, Robbie the toothless old git (T.O.G.), Scottie, The Walkers And Talkers Society (T.W.A.T.S.) - a girlfriend eh??? You won't be allowed out Wednesdays now ha ha ! Big hello's to both Mums, Hazel and Minnie, all at The Gurnards Head, The Tinners Arms and The Bucket of Blood. Love to all more soon.

(Part 2) Steak for dinner tonight - the best yet, but the chocolate chip mousse needs some work! We have settled into our routine of rowing, 16 x 1 hour shifts, and 4 x 2 hour shifts through the night. We now eat breakfast together after the 8am shift. Lunch is after 1pm. Dinner is as the sun sets after the 6pm shift.

Mo has settled down a bit, and calm seas through the night have enabled us to make better progress. We just turned all the boats lights off, and all the majesty of creation was up there in the sky in front of us. Not the sky full of stars like at home, but ten times as many, with shooting stars every little while, including one that was the closest I've ever seen. We watched it burn out almost right down in front of us – brilliant! Funny to see Orion rise here, as I know it is plain right over our back garden gate at home right now. Night is like a magic carpet ride through space, since Mo has calmed down.

From Notebook/log: Mo just got sloppier...and even more sloppier...what a mess of water. Position: 25' 21.747" N, 21' 59.657" W. 1.42 pm.8/12/07.

Sunday 9th December 2007

Paul was pleased today, as we passed within 8 miles of the first waypoint that he worked out back at home – good shot! That having been done, we have resolved to stick to the original route, and go with the wind we've got, which is taking us straight to Antigua.

The sunrise was a beauty again today. No more wild life as yet, but the sky makes up for it. Not just the stars at night, but the clouds during the day – great white fluffy ethereal clouds with every face or animal, mythical or real, in them. They are amazing, and we both love to lie in the cabin, on our off watch, and stare up out of the top hatch. I have never seen anything like them, and there is nobody else here to see them with us. I shall write a poem...or seven! Oh, and Paul saw two UFO's last night, and we both saw weird lights!

12 noon has now passed – so that is one whole week at sea...wow!

Notebook/log: Resolved to go original route, no point rowing 200 miles to find a wind that may not be there, when we've got a friendly one here...that's the logic anyway.

Sunrise WOW!!! Clouds WOW!!! lasting memory. Muesli for brekkers today. No fish or wild life. Hot and sunny. Evening - calmed down

Paul said he saw 2 UFO's last night?? Doesn't sound like Paul..... 1 week at sea... 378 n.m.

Position: 25' 00.479" N, 22' 59.723" W. 1237pm. 9/12/07.

The laptop was plugged into the sat phone via a lead, to send the Blog home. Typing was not easy, everything had three extra "J's", a couple of bogus "P's" and the odd spare "F"!

The first week at sea and we didn't take a lot of pictures

Monday 10th December 2007

A hard night last night. Although calm, we were tired for some reason – can't think why! But today has been just the best day yet – blazing sunshine from sunrise to sunset, (which is just happening as I write this, by the way). Porridge with strawberries is a winner for breakfast.

Mo has been at her calmest yet today, letting us chug across her surface all day with hardly a wave. We have a couple of forthcoming mini landmarks, (or should that be seamarks?), in the next few days, i.e. the 500 mile point to cross, and the Tropics to go into at 23 degrees 27 minutes N.

Some people may be questioning why we are further north than the other boats, well there is a simple answer to that my friends... looking for mackerel, what else!!

Thanks for the messages – keep them coming. Love to friends and families, more blog soon, Steve and Paul.

Notebook/log: Fantastic day, clear blue sky and Mighty Mo is beginning to join in with us. Anyway...it's only north if you view it from the south!

Position: 24 degrees 39.806 minutes N, 23' 47.315" W.1000am. 10/12/07.

The Sam quote of the day (previous 2 days lost in sub-ether somewhere?): "I hate you more...if hate were people, I'd be China!"

Tuesday 11th December 2007

Hi everyone, it's hot...damn hot...I mean its daaaammmmn hot! We've kept plugging away on the oars, which is all we intend to continue doing. We had a tired night and didn't get even the little bit of sleep we needed, but hey, we got over it and we burst into the new day with porridge, twix bars and peanuts...ideal!

Big lobby waves have kept knocking us off course, and The Reason Why steers in this sea, like an old bucking Gloucester bull pig! Talking of pigs, a big mid Atlantic oink from Droops the Watch Pig, who has survived the rough weather so far. He's enjoying himself – and I'm making sure he has plenty of sun cream – nothing worse than a sunburnt snout! Big Hi to everyone in Lostwithiel, Wombwell Homes, Hot Dog, and The Globe – bit short of text messages from you lot, (hint hint), or have you sold my desk and moved ??

Still no sign of wild life, except for Pete the Petrel – I think he's got a thing for Droops!

Notebook/log: Excellent NE tailwind, perfect, flobbing along at 3 knots. Forgot to mention Karen , Richard, the other "Droops" (we won't go into that), and ladies darts team from The Globe. Approaching 500 miles.

Position: 24' 14.885" N, 24' 45.107" W. 1.30pm. 11/12/07

Wednesday 12th December 2007

Do you realise, after such hot days, just how chilly it gets at night? And another thing, why are the nights pitch black, apart from the stars...no moon!! The moon comes up like a Grinning Turk at about 5am, an hour or so before the sun comes up! What's the point of that?

Making progress on another baking hot day, with waves that are not big, but are making it tricky to stay on course....and still no mackerel!!!

We're going to the Tropics now – perhaps they have a moon?

Love to everyone as always Chris, Sam, Bex and Ogz, Dawn, Jake and Danielle. See you all soon.

Position: 23' 47.968"N, 25' 35.169" W. 1210pm. 12/2/07.

The Sam quote of the day, "It is a mistake to try and look too far ahead. The chain of destiny can only be grasped one link at a time"

Thursday 13th December 2007

Several milestones came and went today :- the 500 nautical mile line was crossed, and in the early hours we crossed 23' 27" N, which puts us in the Tropics...yippee!! Still bloody chilly at 4 in the morning though! We also discovered that it is possible to fall asleep whilst rowing!

We must remember to make a sacrifice to Mo, who is being wonderful at the moment, with gentle following seas. We thought a box of Pringles would be a suitable gesture, but then we ate them instead – but we have more! Beautiful days, cloudless, ethereal or otherwise, so hot...strange to think it so cold at home. And Christmas doesn't exist here...bah humbug!!

The Tuna shoal turned up...well, Tommy Tuna did, yes alright it was just the one, but it jumped right out of the water, just as Paul and I looked up. More wildlife arrived later, when a Frigate bird arrived just as I was trying to eat a half hundred weight bag of peanuts. Freddie the Frigate gave us quite a few passes...he must have thought to himself, "couple of old Janners out in a boat...must be some Mackerel about" – too bad Freddie!

Notebook/log: Must get back to me peanuts...have to keep me calories up, I've got a three hundredweight bag to eat before lunch...we're in the Tropics now!

Position: 23' 19.594" N, 26' 17.857" W. 1241pm. 13/12/07.

The Sam quote of the day, "Let me ask you something, if you had to go into battle, would you want him on your side?"

Two Zennor Gig Club rowers, currently lie fourth in the biannual Atlantic Rowing Race, made famous by Olympic gold medallist James Cracknell and TV presenter Ben Fogle. Steve Gardner from Zennor, and Hayle's Paul Harris set off from La Gomera in The Canary Islands in their self built boat, The Reason Why, just over a week ago, and have already completed 370 miles. They hope to take between 50 and 55 days to complete the 2550 nautical mile (2936 miles) trip to the finishing line in Antigua, and raise as much as £25,000 for Cornwall Hospice Care. Their specially designed boat takes its name from a line from Cornwall's unofficial national anthem, Trelawny (Song of The Western Men).

The duo have rowed together for more than 10 years and finished a creditable fifth in the World Pilot Gig Championships at the Isles of Scilly last year. A total of 23 boats set off with 15 competing for the pairs title. Speaking from a satellite phone on board, Steve said the pair were blistered, black and blue from being hit by the oars, but were still laughing. He said, "Last night, we had a good night and rowed right through the night. We did alternate one-hour shifts until midnight, followed by two-hour stints until 8am. and we appear to have made some headway. The wind has dropped a little, but the sea is still choppy and it is hard to put two strokes together."

Supporters can send messages of support at the website www.the-reason-why.co.uk and check progress on the official website at www.atlanticrowingrace2007.co.uk

....

Friday 14th December 2007

A much better night. We ate later and watched the usual rubbish sunrise...that could stop breath...before getting on with the business of making everything hot, sunny and bright. More praise for Mo – the forecast for the next four days is as we are now, which suits us. So, as another dreadful day in paradise without wildlife, heads towards another rubbish sunset, that could also stop breath, we'll say thanks for all the support, including the kind words of Trilby, partner of Chris, who rowed with Clint in "C2" in 2005.

We did make a discovery last night – a distant relative of the Nocturnal La Gomeran Albino Bag Lizard, arrived on the boat...the Nocturnal Mid Atlantic Black Bag Gorilla! He crawls up over the aft cabin after dark, stares at you for 12 hours, then disappears...weird eh? The tropical moon is the same as before, only it comes up before the sun sets, and goes down soon after. Somebody needs to talk job description to these 'ere moons!

The Sam quote of the day, "Only two things are infinite, the Universe and human stupity, and I'm not sure about the former."

More news soon, but in the meantime, another poem, hastily penned, following publication of the first one on the ARR website:-

In The Clouds

They march and dance across the sky

Their poses all in flight

Majestically they float and show

Ethereal delight.

All the faces ever born

Imagined, real or not

Are here for all the world to see

In the land that time forgot.

Notebook/log: Position 22' 49.104" N, 27' 29.135"W. 1.25pm. 14/12/07.

Saturday 15th December 2007

Hi Jen, sorry for the delay in sending our blog entry to you, Mo has been a little temperamental and typing was not an option. Anyway here we go with the weekend progress.

With a messy Mo, and going the wrong way, we tried to strike "a happy medium" and were soon surfing 15 foot waves! We had a disaster tonight...we broke a prong off the eating fork! And since then, we've lost the other two as well!

There are no mornings here, only after nights. We hadn't realised that we would have 13 hours of darkness every day, and only 11 hours of light. By the time you've recovered from the night, it's always afternoon and then it's nearly night again!

Notebook/log: Position: 22' 14.820" N, 27' 58.284" W. 15/12/07. The Nocturnal Mid Atlantic Black Bag Gorilla, is called Gus, by the way.

The Sam quote of the day, "Hey, this is not a test, this is rock and roll! Time to rock it from the Delta to the D.M.Z."

Sunday 16th December 2007

Today, Mo is still messy, but we are going the right way now! We are heading for the second mark which is about 540 miles on, where we can only imagine there is a little roundabout called "Rastus's Place" with one palm tree, a hammock and Rastus rolling a fat one, saying "hey man, this ain't no M25, this is the Tradewinds Freeway, Keep right for Antigua, have a Red Stripe!"

We had a big fry up this morning...well, a boil in the bag up really, then got chased by a couple of angry looking squalls. Fortunately we managed to avoid the worst of them, although a bit of rain was like a welcome shower in this heat. The sweat is running off me as I type this.

Big news, today we saw our first flying fish, a little shoal...or should that be flock? Anyway, we haven't had one in the boat yet. We had a good night on the oars, good Mo and good weather. We had been avoiding eating the wolf fish, as it just didn't sound appealing, but at last I tried some, and guess what....Yep, its bloody awful! I gave mine to Mo...what is Wolf Fish anyway?

Notebook/log: What is Wolf Fish...a howling Mackerel? Gus thinks, for a couple of old raspers, we're moving like a buttered pig, and that's upset Droops, (I must have been wandering a bit when I wrote this, and we definitely hadn't got to the urine drinking stage, either!)

Sea suddenly got big, have to surf with it...another comfortable lunch! Two weeks at sea and didn't even notice it!

Position: 21' 46.160" N, 28' 39.690" W. 1223 pm. 16/12/07.

The Sam quote of the day, "Sixty! We dropped at least sixty, wouldn't you say? That leaves only 3940!"

15Th December – breather

Gus chatting with Droops

Monday 17th December 2007

It has been slow, hot and hard work on the oars today, but we are going the right way. We had an encounter with our fifth tanker ship just now, no radar, no AIS, no "Seame". That's three tankers out of the five that haven't had the equipment they are supposed to have. Anyway, no problems, we've seen them coming and no sweat.

The G.T. Moon (Great Tropical or Grinning Turk!), came along again last night, arriving two hours before the sunset, but it stayed around and lit the night sky up lovely. At one point it hung in the sky golden, with a scallop out of the top side and it looked for the world like The Holy Grail! I was ready to forgive it all, until the daft sod went down at 1.17am, leaving us nearly seven hours of night as black as pitch.

F.A.O. Amanda: Can Woodvale do something about this rebellious moon situation?? Or are they on a three day week?

More soon, when Mo and the charging laptop allow. Love to all and thanks for the tremendous support – it's been a bit overwhelming really...but please don't stop!!

Notebook/log: Position: 21' 09.129" N, 29' 21.209" W. 1.40pm. 17/12/07.

The Sam quote of the day, "Youth cannot know how age thinks and feels. But old men are guilty if they forget what it was to be young."

Tuesday 18th December 2007

I have to start with an erratum (things I got wrong last time):- the frigate bird I referred to wasn't, it was a red billed tropical bird, but funnily enough, it's name was still Freddie! Secondly, and someone should have noticed this, on Rastus's island, what's the use of a hammock with only one palm tree??

Today was the calmest day so far with no wind, no Mo, no sound, no wildlife...nothing...if I can get Paul to stop singing a medley of "The Lonely Goatherd", "I'd like to teach the world to sing", "Down at the tube station at midnight" and "Is this the way to Amarillo!!"It will be lovely! Very hot again today and trying to make progress against the sea was hard work. Paul took the opportunity to clean the bottom of the boat – I'm not ready for this adventure yet. As Paul said, its four and a half miles deep and it would take a cannonball, one hour forty minutes to hit the bottom....how does anybody know that??

The old Grinning Turk moon was at it again last night but the stars and the shooting stars are incredible. Several people have asked for more poetry – those who know me will tell you thats a silly thing to do!

The Sam quote of the day, "Police arrested two kids yesterday, one was drinking battery acid, the other was eating fireworks. They charged one, and let the other off"

A Thousand Million Stars of Light

All of God's creation

Is looking down on me

A thousand million stars of light

On us upon the sea

The waves provide the music

In this cathedral of the night

For shooting stars and meteors

And the moon gone out of sight

All of God's creation

Is looking down on me

Perhaps we'll find "The Reason Why"

As we go across the sea

Notebook/log: The Grinning Turk did the Holy Grail thing again, but later. If it carries on, should have full moonlit sky in six days! Wind light, but turned against us. No people...haven't seen a soul in 2 weeks...weird! Beginning to think we need to turn radically South, our plan isn't really working, wind and sea not going with us now, maybe a bit late, but hey...

Wind got up, fairly wild old night, but rowed through ok, had done 30nm. by 8am.

No Position

By Jen.

I have just phoned "The Reason Why" for the first time, and am not looking forward to the phone bill now! Anyway, all is well on board, and both Paul and Steve are in fine spirits, although the temperature inside the cabin is 83', and that's with both hatches open! Having gone in the wrong direction recently, they are back on course but are experiencing some headwinds which probably won't affect the boats further South. They are therefore expecting their mileage to drop for the next few days. They have today given the hull a clean off, as there was enough wildlife attached underneath to slow up their progress.

They both have sore backs and bottoms although nothing too severe, but their hands are holding up very well. Oh, and sore feet where the straps keep rubbing, even though they are wearing shoes. Expectations before setting out on this row were that there would be more extremes of conditions, i.e. some very flat days and some much rougher days, but they seem to be experiencing lots of medium rough days which make it uncomfortable, and provide enough movement that you can't stand up or put a cup of tea down anywhere, or it will be gone. Generally speaking, it is hard work, but nothing worse than expected, and they are enjoying it.

The days go past quite quickly, but the nights seem to take forever because it gets dark before 7pm, and does not get light again until 8am. During their rest periods, they have to eat, sleep, plot charts, wash etc so it never seems long before its time to take to the oars again. They are very pleased with the progress they making, especially considering they are not all out racing, and still stop to eat together for a while for breakfast, dinner and tea. Their main priority remains to make it safe and sound to the other side of The Atlantic, as quickly as they can, but without taking risks, or making it any harder than it is already. They are all very civilised on "The Reason Why". No sightings of anybody else, boats, support vessels etc since leaving La Gomera, although they did see a tanker recently, that was a bit close for comfort..

Talking of comfort, I asked if there was anything they needed, meaning info or bearings etc, they answered, "some new forks and two pints of beer!"

They are extremely pleased to know that their website is receiving so many hits, and that friends and supporters have recently donated more money to their chosen charity, Cornwall Hospice Care, via Paypal. The amount of supporters and well wishers is quite amazing and has far exceeded their expectations.

Wednesday 19th December 2007

We have turned South at last, it was a wild old night but have finally got beyond the 20th parallel, and seem to be in the Trades. We reckon only a mere 1805 nautical miles to go" There are no waves here, just monstrous mountainsides of water, but they are going our way thank goodness.

As we get on with our journey south and west, there is one final thing to report. The great dunker biscuit robbery for which the prime suspect is Gus The Black Bag Gorilla – we hadn't got any fresh lycees you see. If it turns out to be Gus, this will damage his chances of a romantic liaison with Griselda, the other Black Bag Gorilla frequenting the "Keira Knightly Suite" (alias the forward cabin)

For Robbie, you toothless old git, put your reply address in the text message, and I will try and reply, got no number here, thanks mate. More soon, love to all Steve and Paul.

Notebook/log: Now going South and West, but they are not waves here, but whole moving mountainsides of water of unstoppable force 40, 50 maybe 60 feet high, and you just have to go with them, or you don't go at all. Although we do have to go slightly across them to stay on course, but so far so good!

Porridge and strawberries again today, have GPS bearing on finish line, 1805 nm. hey, it's closer than it was!

Position: 19' 54.669" N, 30' 13.331" W. 1200 noon. 19/12/07

Sam quote of the day got through, after a few days when it didn't:- "Eternal nothingness is fine if you happen to be dressed for it!"

Thursday 20th December 2007

It lashed down with rain all last night, and we did not think for one moment about the 27 odd revellers from Zennor Gig Club, eating chicken and chips washed down with beer and blackberry wine, in The Waterside Meadery, Penzance!! What would we do with chicken and chips, when we've got dried Aardvark and essence of dead dog to eat (and that bloody Wolf Fish!)? Mind you, at 0410am. the thought "I hope it chokes them" did randomly flit across my mind...but not for long, good turnout chaps!

Notebook/log: Two flying fish just glided past the boat, 2 inches above the waves, then disappeared in unison...magic. We are well in the semi-trades now, making 3-3.5 knots at present, sea not too big, just your average three storey house size!

No position today, apparently there is another article in The Cornishman again.

The Sam quote of the day, "I wish you'd help a bit, you're always refurbishing yourself."

ROWERS SECOND

The Cornishman Newspaper – 20th December 2007

Zennor Gig rowers Steve Gardner and Paul Harris have moved up into second place in the cross Atlantic rowing race, made famous two years ago by Olympian James Cracknell and TV presenter Ben Fogle. The pair who both row for Zennor Gig Club, have covered more than 700 miles of the route between The Canaries and Antigua, in their boat "The Reason Why", and trail the leaders by more than a day.

Supporters can check progress on the website at www.atlanticrowingrace2007.co.uk

....

Friday 21st December 2007

A rough, blowey and choppy night – I may never sit still again – and I'm sure my first meal on land will get thrown all over the floor!

Message to Trilby, don't worry, we had a good talk to Gus, and tempted him with chocolate biscuits last night, and he passed the test, so it's up to the Keira Knightly Suite with Griselda, for Gus!

We now have 142 jobs for a calm day, as we haven't had one yet, we need a week of them to get everything done! Every morning as the sun rises, and I emerge from the cabin hatch and proclaim "It's a new Dawn!" with hope anew etc, as the heater slowly rises and restores her warmth to this wet world. It reminds me of a Douglas Adams passage, from "Hitch-Hikers", "Each morning the sun drags herself up over the horizon, hauls herself across the sky, spreading a little warmth here, casting a little light there, and then sadly sinks below the opposite horizon, eleven hours later, with a feeling of totally wasted effort!"

Hey Amanda, the moon stayed up until 4am - ish – have you pulled rank?

Right, must go and put some sun cream on Droops snout...he's fading!

Notebook/log: Each morning I spring from the cabin, through the hatch to proclaim "A New Dawn!"

"Woke up this morning" on full blast for the 20th time, just has to be done every morning (theme from The Sopranos...it works).

Position: 18' 43.300" N, 31' 46.130"W. 1208am. 21/12/07

The Sam quote of the day, "I'm like a cat here, a no name slob. We belong to nobody, and nobody belongs to us. We don't even belong to each other."

Saturday 22nd December 2007

We are bouncing along the Atlantic Highway today – not exactly comfortable but going the right way! Night comes so often here, there is no morning or afternoon, just after-night, and pre-night.

New development – I am writing this very quietly as we believe The Reason Why is haunted ... every time we glance into one of the hatches, we see an apparition of an old, tired eyed, sad faced gentleman with a bushy beard. We've both seen him, and funnily enough, he looks familiar to us both somehow!

Just a note about the start: Bill, one of the South Africans, is also a mad Douglas Adams fan, and had asked for boat no.42. Unfortunately for him, we got there first, but the last words anyone said to me in La Gomera were from Bill, which he shouted across the start line to me, as I was reciting my prayer to Mo, "So Long and thanks for all the fish" which is another D.A. book. But in the Hitch Hikers Guide to The Galaxy, who can tell me who, or what said these words in the book?

Hi to Richard and Graham at The Tinners, thanks for the message. Hi to all at The Gurnards Head, Charles, Andy, Rachel, Krish, Ogz of course, and everyone else. Robbie and Scottie, thanks for the messages. The other T.W.A.T.S. JL, thanks for the chart, Colin ... be good! (The Walkers and Talkers Society, we walk between pubs across the moors!)

Merry Christmas to everyone, especially families gathering without us. See you all soon.

Notebook/log: Position:18' 19.300" N, 32' 43.263" W. 1324 pm. 22/12/07.

The Sam quote of the day, "How does he find his way in the dark?" "He "thinks" his way, a lot of people think they're telepathic." "OOOh God I hate the bush!"

Sunday 23rd December 2007

Notebook/log: Position: 17' 59.996" N, 33' 49.084"W.   no time 23/12/07

Sam quote of the day, "Are you sure there are two L's in dollar, Gideon?" "Aye, and there's two G's in bugger off!"

Monday 24th December 2007

Plodding on and reached the 1000 mile marker – very good of Woodvale to put a neon palm tree in the middle of Mo to tell us. Rumour has it that this palm tree is the estranged one missing from Rastus Island, but that's just a bit of mid Atlantic gossip.

After rowing all day, we decided to start tapping the weevils out of the boat's biscuits ready for tomorrow's lunch. Then I wrote a poem just for Keith:-

Christmas On The Atlantic

It's Christmas on The Atlantic

The wave tops white as snow

And they bounce and they roll and they fizzle

At the will of Mighty Mo

The Christmas lights were missing

No holly or a tree

But I wore a big red Santa coat

Cos the bugger rained on me!

It's Christmas on The Atlantic

And it's not the same as land

Cos peace and still and silent nights

Mo just can't understand

Notebook/log: Christmas Eve...odd! Phoned Chris, Listening to Foo Fighters, Eagles and Richard Ashcroft. Allowed half a jaffa cake each!

Position: 17' 52.624"N, 34' 40.349W. 1724. 24/12/07.

The Sam quote of the day "The ultimate measure of a man, is not where he stands in moments of comfort and convenience, but where he stands at times of challenge and controversy."

Tuesday 25th December 2007 – Christmas Day

We ate the weevils – they were better than the biscuits! MERRY CHRISTMAS everyone, and thanks for the hundreds of text messages – sorry we can't answer them all.

We opened our boxes from home, which included three miniature Southern Comforts (take note, I like this if the beers off!), three ports, red wine, champagne and rum. Are they making a statement do you think?

We had an incident in the early hours of Christmas morning – the "Seame" and radar alarms started sounding, and there was our sixth tanker, the "Hoegh Sydney" doing 17.8 knots, and coming within 4 miles of us. It looked nearer as we watched it go past at 0330am. We had our favourite steak boil in a bag, drank rum, rowed....the usual sort of Christmas – not! Mo allowed us a very calm Christmas night which was nice. So many messages from home, thank you all so much. We'll try not to let you down.

Notebook/log: Fry up, Fairings, Apricots, prunes, chocolate, rum, photos. Time zones out by two hours...got up too early!! Put tinsel on Droops. Spoke to all on phone. Great steak and potato dinner. Wind going east...what a weird Christmas! It's Christmas Jim but not as we know it! Thought I'd write a poem sitting here, eating second half of jaffa cakes from yesterday. The old Grinning Turk came out and it was really enjoyable. God love everyone for their support, apparently no work is going on in Cornwall, and even the beer sales are slow, so many following our blog/dot. No Position today... day off

The Sam quote of the day, Hi Dad and Paul, Merry Christmas. Just off to the Tinners and will take a drink or two for you both. Thanks for the presents, Baggins is going nuts, I don't think he had a stroke, more like he's a puppy again! Amazing progress and 1000n.miles down. Surely you can see Antigua now? The quote is quite apt today, keep it up and look forward to speaking to you soon, - "Again the ghost sped on, above the black and heaving sea – on, on, until being far away from any shore, they lighted on a ship. They stood beside the helmsman at the wheel, the lookout in the bow, the officers who had the watch; dark ghostly figures in their several stations, but every man among them hummed a Christmas tune, or had a Christmas thought, or spoke below his breath to his companion of some bygone Christmas Day, with homeward hopes belonging to it. And every man on board, waking or sleeping, good or bad, had had a kinder word for another on that day, than on any other day of the year; and had shared to some extent in its festivities; and had remembered those he cared for at a distance, and had known that they had delighted to remember him."

Wednesday 26th December 2007

We had an early visit from Trinni and Tobago – the two very nice Tropical birds who popped by to see if we were interested in the job on Rastus Island, as second palm tree, or if it looks better on the passport, Hammock holder first class. I respectfully declined, saying we were on route for Antigua. "Too busy for me" said Trinni, "full of touristy seagulls!"

The calm weather continues, very calm, it's like rowing an old Gloucester sow up hill through treacle. This is not a buttered pig situation, but at night, the old Grinning Turk moon quickly became a star, if that's possible? He illuminated the otherwise inky blackness, by fighting his way through a million freshly baked harvest loaves, a three square mile Bakewell Tart, a fish the size of Cornwall, and a three hundred foot rampaging stallion in full gallop ... at least that's what the amazing cloud cover looked like. He then shone a moonlight trail on our exact course – it was pretty special.

Notebook/log: Riding the Moonlight Trail, as the sun sets behind us over the bow, the Grinning Turk is beating back the clouds in his path, to come up astern, casting a bright moonlight trail to follow, after 2 hours of inky blackness, where we don't know where the hell we are!

Position: 17' 36.900" N, 36' 11,168" W. 1230pm. 26/12/07.

The Sam quote of the day, "I was pissing by the door, when I heard two shats. You are holding in your hand a smoking goon; you are clearly the guilty potty!"

Christmas ... bah humbug!

Thursday 27th December 2007

Still no wind, heavy old Mo, backs and bums suffering, but the cheese melts are good, and unlike Captain Jack Sparrow, we still have the rum!

On a whim, Paul decided to go fishing last night with his £1.75 hand line from Lidl's. From the decision to fish, dropping the line, catching fish, losing fish, catching second fish, filleting fish, frying and eating fish – half hour tops, so no problems for fish out here. I don't know what it was, but it was bright shiny yellow with a blue tail, and it tasted good.

Today is day 25 and mileage wise we are heading for halfway hopefully by New Year, then hopefully a bit quicker run in, but we'll see.

Notebook/log: Position: 17' 32.011"N, 36' 11.168"W. 1118am. 27/12/07

The Sam quote of the day, "If my calculations are correct, when this baby hits eighty-eight miles per hour, you're gonna see some serious shit!"

Friday 28th December 2007

Still no wildlife apart from Pete the Petrel, who sometimes brings a mate. There is also the fish ... "Dorado" I think, or is that beer? They follow the boat, and at night, catch in the lights of our head lamps, flashing like a silver blue ballet all around us, and with every oar stroke tumbling over a myriad tiny phosphorescent jewels ... I feel a poem coming on ... but not today.

Notebook/log: Very hot, long slow haul across Mo, heading for halfway marker, and excitingly, we are now on the Antigua side of the chart, and La Gomera on the other. Still a way to go mind. Only tiny flying fish on the boat so far.

Position: 17' 29.130" N, 37' 48.507" W. 5.10pm. 28/12/07

The Sam quote of the day, Max, "give me the star charts", David, "not now I gotta go", Max, "go where?" David, "to the bathroom", Max, "don't know bathroom?"

Saturday 29th December 2007

A Day In The Life ...

12 Midnight – Steve 2 hour row. Paul - eat, sleep, repair bum

0200 - Paul 2hour row (if I can wake him!). Steve – eat, sleep, repair bum

0400 Steve collapse in a heap, try and wake Paul and 0600 ditto in reverse.

Change over banter - I say old chap, it's 2hrs and it's your turn. No problem, the alarm went off ok, and I'm fully awake and ready to go. You get some sleep, see you in a couple of hours...good night.

Actual – "uh..um..ba, bloody hell..er late, bwaph, ooh bum..ma um""

0800 – Steve 1 hour row. Paul 1st breakfast, muesli, go bar, biscuits tea.

0900 – Paul 1 hour row. Steve 1st breakfast, apple and custard, biscuits coffee.

1000 – 1800 Alternate 1 hour rows, snacks and stretches, write blog, repairs, naps, listen to music, lunches are individual, we make ourselves after a row usually 1400-1500. Make water, top up water container, plot position, raid snack bucket.

1800 – Sundowner, Reason Why free drinks club, drink a tot of rum and watch the sun set together for about half an hour. The highlight of our day.

1830 – 1900 alternate who does the extra half hour. Get an oink out of Droops.

1900 – 2400, back on hourly rota till midnight. Cook individual dinner after one of the evening rows, usually 2100 or 2200.

12 Midnight - Start again!

I like to play "Woke up his Morning", by The Alabama 3 (theme from The Sopranos) every morning, as I emerge from the cabin to proclaim, "A New Dawn!" As I've said before, and I think I spring out cheerily like a butterfly from a cocoon, but my mate reckons it's more like a dung beetle from a turd!

The only other thing worthy of a mention in the daily routine, besides trying to write this blog in a revolving sauna, is ... the bucket!! At some stage during the day, at least once, we have to become performing monkey acrobats and magicians, as in turn, we have to perch precariously on a plastic bucket, steering the foot steering with one hand, hang on to the boat with the other hand, and hang on to the bucket with your thighs. And all the while you are trying to concentrate on the job in hand, so to speak, Mo tries her damnest to throw us off the bucket, and the bucket off the boat! It is slightly easier if your mate is awake, as he can steer for you.

We then track the Grinning Turk across the sky, if he bothers to turn up, last night he came up at 0230am.

Notebook/log: Tiny breeze but swelteringly hot, still plodding to halfway, on schedule pre-31 December. Hopefully find some wind then and skedaddle to Antigua. Wind picked up afternoon, better progress, and Grinning Turk grinned at us the entire night!

Position: 17' 29.022" N, 38' 18.723" W. 1.42pm. 29/12/07.

The Sam quote of the day, "All you need is trust, and a little bit of Pixie dust!"

Sunday 30th December 2007

At midday today, we have been at sea for four weeks, (how is that possible?), and we haven't seen another living soul since – weird!! We were cast adrift in a 23 foot open boat with no cold drinks only salty water, no cheese or ham, (the first items in the menu of international cuisine), no chocolate or sweets (we forgot to buy any in La Gomera!), and the plastic cutlery that we have (which was only supposed to be in reserve but we forgot the proper stuff!), is rapidly running out of prongs. Hence our forks are now more like spoons – just as well because we broke the spoons!! Oh for bread and a pork pie, oh perishable substance we covet thee!! But unlike Jack Sparrow, we have still got the rum!!

Notebook/log: The elusive halfway marker still eludes us by 36 miles or so. Miss those beautiful fresh oranges we brought from La Gomera, or a pasty ... we'd kill for one! Wind in wrong direction this morning, going across it ok though. Hot again ... shoals of Dorado follow the boat at night, shining/flashing blue and silver, and the tiny shiny beads of phosphorescence – beautiful. Bigger fish seem to chase the flying fish – nearly had a flying fish in the ear last night!

Position: 17' 13.416" N, 38' 57.486" W. 1250pm. 30/12/07.

The Sam quote of the day, "When was the last time you were home?" "Two years, two hundred and sixty-four days and this morning."

Monday 31ˢᵗ December 2007

Those ghostly old apparitions seem to be looking even older and they still hang about in the hatch covers. We got to the elusive halfway point today, apparently, although there is some confusion over the mileage. Poem time...

Every

Every stroke is 10 yards further

Every wave is 10 yards more

Every breeze is 10 yards nearer

Every day is nearer shore.

Every second brings us closer

Every minute on the foam

Every time we travel forward

Every yard is nearer home.

sg 16 nov 2007

Notebook/log: We think we're over the halfway mark, now approaching 1300 miles rowed, so 3 weeks is possible for the 50 day target, God and Mo willing. Need some inspiration till the 1500 mile marker, so will put every stroke poem here. No position today.

The Sam quote of the day, "All we have to decide is what to do with the time that is given to us."

Tuesday 1ˢᵗ January 2008

All is quiet on New Years Day. Mo has let us go a little quicker and although baking hot, we are making all speed to get to the 1000 miles to go mark.

Happy New Year to everyone, especially our families and the thousands of people following our progress. Can't type much more now - very difficult to type in this bear pit of a cabin.

Notebook/log: Haven't seen a living soul for 4 weeks, last ship was Christmas night 1 week ago. Phoned home and Mum. Chris has booked hotel in Antigua, "Ocean Inn" most of other choices fully booked. Sam and Alex managed to get in "The Copper and Lumber Company", Dawn got Paul and family in "The Admirals Inn" which was full when we phoned, but must have had a cancellation, before Dawn rang.

Position: 16' 55.184" N, 40' 27.434" W. 1.48pm. 01/01/08

The Sam quote of the day, "Try not? Do or do not, there is no try!"

Wednesday 2ⁿᵈ January 2007

Hello everybody. Mo is on form, but the Trade Winds are blowing so mustn't grumble. Typing very difficult, and stifling hot in cabin. Notebook/log: Very big sea, 15 – 20 knot wind all day. Ploughed on through, no position. Sam's quote of the day, "You've seen a ship with black sails that's crewed by the damned, and captained by a man so evil, Hell itself spat him back out."

Thursday 3ʳᵈ January 2008 – by Jen

I have today heard from The Reason Why, that the support yacht "Sara" has paid a visit to Paul and Steve this morning. The guys were very pleased to see some new faces - for the first time in four weeks!

The support crew took some photos, which will hopefully be published on the ARR website soon, so keep a look out. I have just received copies so will put in here too.

When "Sara" left The Reason Why, she was off to find "No Fear", and Paul and Steve were quite sad to see her sail off.

Notebook/log: Sea not as big as yesterday, but wind not quite East enough. Visit from Stu on "Sara", couldn't believe it when I saw the mast coming up behind us. Had to talk them in close by radio, sea too big, they couldn't see us from a quarter mile away! Great to have a chat, they came close enough to talk without radios, first people we'd seen in 4 weeks let alone speak to! They took some photos. After the scant and limited rations we had been on, we were obviously extremely sympathetic when Stu told us how tough it had been for them, since their bread maker packed up!!! Also, the dried/rehydrated food gives me heartburn quite bad, and I am eating Gaviscon tablets like Smarties! What we wouldn't do for bread or a pasty!

Quite sad to see them go, but resolved to make it spur us on. Rigged up second rowing position to go two up, to get back up to 17'N and below the 1000 miles point.

"Sara"   trying to photograph the ghost!

The Sam quote of the day, "First, you must find me....... another shrubbery!"

Friday 4th January 2008

Notebook/log: Less than 100 miles to the 1000 to go marker. Three weeks is still possible, weather and sea permitting. My Arse! Trinni and Toby came back today... why Toby, should be Suzannah! (I went for Trinidad and Tobago, not Trinni and Suzannah!)

Position: 16' 57.241" N, 43' 11.187" W.   3.50pm.   04/01/08, and just to prove it...

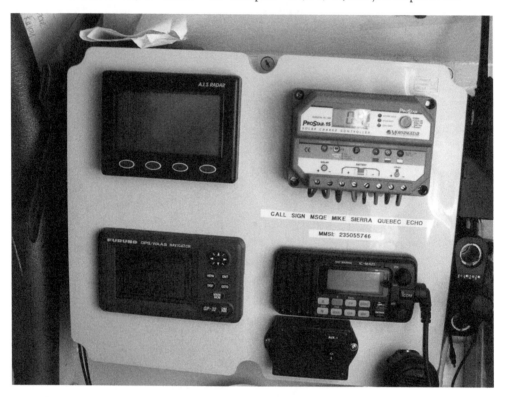

..well, you might just be able to see the read out on the GPS, bottom left.

The Sam quote of the day, "I am not a vigilante, I am just trying to get home to my little girl's birthday party, and if everyone will just stay out of my way, nobody will get hurt!"

Saturday 5th January 2008

Notebook/log: Calm, hot, still. Sorted food out, see what we had left and re packed with the nicer stuff on top! Passed 1500 miles rowed, 1030 to go. Paul cleaned bottom of boat, but not bad.

The Sam quote of the day, "I tried to think of the most harmless thing. Something that could never ever possibly destroy us...Mr. Stay Puft!"

Position: 16' 57.387"N, 43' 50.353" W.   1400. 05/01/08.

Hi all! This is the updated blog since 2nd Jan. Sorry for the delay. We have now been at sea for five weeks. Since the big seas and strong winds of 2nd Jan, Mo has sort of calmed down a bit, although the wind and sea seem to be at odds and not in our favour, hence the struggle to get past the 1000 mile to go marker, which we finally did at 0630 today. Yesterday was very hot, so Paul had a look at TRY's bottom while the sea was calm. Nothing much on it, but we like to keep our bottoms clean! It is our bottoms giving us the most grief and discomfort at the moment, and every time one of us finishes rowing, the other is greeted by a "Jim Royal" "my arse!" We've had visits from Trinni and Toby, the tropical birds and "Sara" the support yacht, which was great. They stayed for about 20 minutes, took some photos and then sailed off to the next boat.

Picture this, a man just awoken from an attempt at sleep, just sitting on the rowing seat, when a great slapper of a wave hits the side of the boat and soaks him all over. It was 2.15am straight after a rain storm the like of which you've never seen descended upon him, and you can understand what dejected means. But I got over it!

The old Grinning Turk is up to his tricks again, and is now only a slither of his former self, but the idiot didn't rise until 6am ... just before the sun! As we continue plodding on towards Antigua, here's another poem, inspired by my daughter Rebecca...

The Problem With The Land

There isn't any water

And everywhere's so still

Where's the fun in drinking tea

That you never get to spill

All your clothes are dry not damp

Your towel is never wet

There's room to wash, and nasty spots

You hardly ever get

There's space you can stand up in

Without a smack on head

You don't have to scramble through a hatch

And there's room for two in bed

There's people you can talk to

Or visit them by car

Or even walk there using legs

But maybe that's too far

So what's land got to offer

Cities, trees and sand

But it hasn't got an ocean

That's the problem with the land

Love to families and friends, and thank you for the hundreds and thousands of messages. Notebook/log: Mo turned uppity later and wind wrong. Position: 16' 57.346" N, 44'42.565" W. 1547. 06/01/08

Managed to pour boiling water down my leg instead of in the food packet, but leaped up and dunked leg in sea water, and it never blistered and hardly left a mark, lucky really.

The Sam quote of the day, "Make it so number one!"

Monday 7th January 2008

Notebook/log: Good day and night, except it's Port for our Sundowner tot each night now, as the rum has gone!!

Position:16' 57.273" N, 45' 32.979" W. 6.15pm. 07/01/08

The Sam quote of the day, "just one chance to come back here and tell our enemies that they may take our lives, but they will never take our freedom!"

Tuesday 8th January 2008

Notebook/log: Over 54 miles last night and so far today. Wind and Mo going East. Now 896 miles to go. No Grinning Turk for two nights now. Dawn broke to The Foo Fighters. Good news, we found porridge and strawberries hidden away and tins of ham etc. Thought we'd eaten them all. Tins of ham with super noodles or baked beans and sausages in tomato sauce and super noodles, were winners for our lunches.

Position: 16' 57.182"N, 46' 35.548" W. 2033. 08/01/08

Disaster the rum has officially gone!!

The Sam quote of the day, "If you build it, he will come."

Wednesday 9th January 2008

Notebook/ log: Going ok, sea good at times, all east – phew! It sometimes goes all thick and heavy like treacle, very hard to row and frustrating as it seems to slow up progress markedly. Other times, when we get out of the treacly bits...we fly! Very temperamental Mo. We are panicking a bit now, as we know our families are booking flights, and will start arriving in Antigua 19 – 21 January, and our biggest fear is of missing them!!! My rough guide to the last 850 miles...

9/1 10/1 11/1 12/1 13/1 14/1 15/1 16/1 17/1 18/1 19/1 20/1 21/1 22/1 23/1 24/1 25/1

850 800 750 699 650 599 550 500 450 400 350 300 250 200 150 100 50

Based on my average of 50 miles a day, we should arrive on 26th Jan, wind and Mo permitting, which although not perfect, we will take very gladly.

Satellite phone is playing up again. Position: 16' 57.284" N, 47' 22.175" W. 7pm. 9/1/08

Sam quote of the day, "Go on, lean in. Listen, you hear it? ... Carpe... hear it? ...Carpe... Carpe Diem .. seize the day boys, make your lives extraordinary."

Thursday 10th January 2008

Notebook/log: Grinning Turk still away. Rain, a thick black night, no stars. Wind got up, sluggish over night, but then moving better, before turning sluggish and treacly again. Clouds cleared day, baking hot again. 46 miles for 750 to go. Got L and R (left and right) crosstrack error mixed up on course setting GPS, difficult in sea and cross wind, energy sapping rowing the wrong way to get back on course, I got a bit (actually a lot!) annoyed with it!! Grinning Turk up as new moon sliver, funny sluggish sea, like rowing through a mixture of treacle and tarmac!

Sam quote of the day, "You're gonna eat lightnin' and you're gonna crap thunder!"

Jethro's Japanese Admiral is alive and well and currently Mid Atlantic!

Friday 11th January 2008

Hi everyone, been a bit busy on the oars lately to be able to write a blog. We've been making up a few miles, but Between Mo and the wind, they conspire to make life difficult. The cunning old Grinning Turk has been playing away and we haven't seen him for a few nights, until last night, when a mere slither of a thing appeared and cast very little light as we hurtled backwards into the inky black void. Big black clouds rained on us in the wee small hours as well. On top of everything else ... the rum has gone!!

We had a very frustrating night last night, making all speed for the 750 n/miles to go mark, but wind and sea delayed us. We are, at this moment, within 4 miles of it, at 11.35am local time (1.35pm with you).

Now we don't want to tempt fate, but the facts are, that family accommodation is either being, or has been booked in Antigua, so there were a few minor requests to be taken into consideration, which have been sent home for when choosing the hotel, or whatever:-

1. No amusements, fairs or games that involve too much random movement. Definitely no gym with rowing machines. Nowhere with a hatch or alarm clocks.

2. No food out of bags, no food or drink you add water too, no bloody noodles on the menu. No laptops that bounce up and down uncontrollably. Nothing salty, especially water, in fact...no water!

3. No so-called hi-tech equipment that keeps you awake all night bleeping, for no good reason. No damp towels or damp clothes. No headlamps. No large buckets. No refillable drinking bottles.

4. No wet toilet paper. No forks without prongs and no spoons with prongs. No GPS cross track error, in fact nothing with an "L" or "R" on it.

5. No fully inclusive outings, especially NO BLOODY BOAT TRIPS, and finally NO SEA VIEW. I will pay for the grottiest back yard with rubbish bins and a scabby dog chasing a scabby cat. Other than that ... I'm easy!

My turn on the oars, so better go and take over from Paul. Thanks again for all your texts and support, sorry if not many get answered. Love to family and friends, we really do hope to see you soon now. Love Steve and Paul

Sorry Jen, forgot to say Hi, here's the blog. x

The Sam quote of the day, "I have no idea to this day what those two Italian ladies were singing about. Truth is, I don't want to know. Some things are best left unsaid."

Saturday 12th January 2008

Notebook/log: Bad night!! (What I actually wrote was far more agricultural than that). I think this would have to be our low point. Our families are going to be in Antigua very soon, and definitely some days at least before us. This is putting pressure on us and making us a little fractious, and truth be known, we are beginning to look forward to finishing now. The weather isn't helping, by turning nasty and uncooperative, and the sea unpredictable. Turning from clean and smooth to treacle, and back again constantly, making for frustratingly slow progress, for the same maximum effort.

Position: 17' 02.045"N, 49' 14.906" W. 1030am. 12/01/08

The Sam quote of the day, "God, I'd give anything for a drink. I'd give my God-damned soul for just a glass of beer."

Sunday 13th January 2008

Notebook/log: Progress a bit better but not much, plenty of sea going sort of our way, so we are pushing hard.686 miles to go. Tanker no.7 appeared, literally we saw it before the "Sea-me" or AIS radar told us she was there. Crossing the New York-Rio shipping lane now, so could be some traffic about. This one was called "Pawtra Naree" whatever that is, according to the AIS.

At noon we will have been at sea for six weeks, and I simply cannot believe or understand this time and where it all has gone. Hard night on oars, went 2 up to try and push on, exhausted, asleep at oars, but not far off my schedule so has to be done. Went naked rowing, couldn't bear the rub of shorts, undercarriage a sea of red spots and open sores, sorry, but never had discomfort like it.

The Sam quote of the day, "Have you ever danced with the Devil in the pale moonlight?"

No Position

Monday 14th January 2008

Notebook/log: Heading for 500 miles out on Wednesday if possible...Naked again, kind of liberating and more comfortable, not sure Paul agrees!! "Twilight Dunkers!" The Sam quote of the day, "I've seen things you people wouldn't believe. Attack ships on fire off the shoulder of Orion." No Position.

Tuesday 15th January 2008

Notebook/log: Naked again...good night – 588 miles to go. Early morning very hot. Grinning Turk up early and down early! Rang Home and Mum. Nick rang from "No Fear" they sound a bit low, they've had enough, be glad to get there now...won't we all.

Position: 17' 03.545" N, 51' 38.982" W. 1357. 15/01/08.

The Sam quote of the day, "Anyone else would have left you by now, but I'm sticking with you. And if I have to ride your ass like Zorro, you're going to show me the money."

Wednesday 16th January 2008

Sorry for delay since last blog, but we've had a couple of bad nights, and mileage has suffered and we've been trying to catch up. Seem to have got through it now and wind and sea, sort of in our favour now, better than before anyway. We have passed the 600 n/miles to go and have rowed 2002 n/miles. Closing in on 500 n/mile and should reach it by late today or early tomorrow.

We've had a brush with a couple more tankers, no. 7 was in broad daylight, but we didn't see him till he was level with us! Tanker no.8 was actually a cruise ship that came up on our tail, so to speak, last night. A mass of lights it was. It was called "Black Watch" according to the AIS, and I called up the Captain, who was a splendid fellow, who took our website address, and slowed down to put powerful spotlights on us. He then announced us to the passengers who nearly tipped the thing over coming to one side to look at us. He wished us good luck in getting to Antigua, and promised to look the website up.

Last Sunday saw us at sea for 6 weeks – don't ask me how that's possible or where the time's gone. Important news is, that we've found choccy biscuits tucked away in one of the more difficult compartments to get at, and have introduced twilight dunking, which of course avoids meltage! We now look forward to our twilight dunk since the rum has gone – had I mentioned that the rum had gone?

Not that you really want to know, but I've gone naked rowing a few days now. It just had to be done if you'd seen my backside! Luckily with a physique very similar to James Cracknell, it hopefully isn't that unpleasant, and with therapy Paul should eventually recover!

On the wildlife front, things have been a bit sparse, but picked up about 20 minutes ago when two whales, possibly Pilot Whales, came and frightened the life out of me by surfacing and blowing a spout of water from their blow holes about ten yards from me. They were gone before Paul could get the camera, unfortunately. Yes, it's poetry time again, and when not rowing or on deck, (that's promenade or poop!), this is where we inevitably are:-

The Bear Pit

It may not have a pretty door

Or curtains round the hatch

It may not have a window box

Or roof tiles, slate or thatch

It may not have a garden

Or flowers planted bright

It hasn't got a dining room

Or one small table light

But this place is our home now

And has been seven weeks

We christened it "The Bear Pit"

Because it simply reeks

Clothes stand up without us

Towels crack when folded down

The mattresses once brightly blue

Have all turned beastly brown

In daytime it's a sauna

In night time it's "The Pit"

Strewn about with sweaty clothes

From two old beastly gits

But She has been our haven

Gainst tempest, wave and gale

And we both know our "Bear Pit"

Would us never ever fail

It may not have a pretty door

It may not smell that sweet

But all who enter, never fear

No safer place you'll meet

That's it. Love to families , friends and supporters, we shouldn't be long now... if I can just stop Paul singing and get him rowing, we'd be laughing!

Notebook/log: After sent blog re. whales, a shark came up to the boat and followed for a minute or two, (about 6-7 foot long) too quick for photo again. Heading for 500 mark ... got there 0816, but it has been an awful night, sloppy sea against us. 498 miles to go Position: 17' 00.056" N, 52' 28.652" W.   1205. 16/01/08.

The Sam quote of the day, "What is it you want, Mary? What do you want? You want the moon? Just say the word and I'll throw a lasso around it and pull it down."

Thursday 17th January 2008

Notebook/log only: Ok...flowing along all day, early 480 miles to go, 6pm 430 miles to go... on schedule. Tanker/container ship no. 9, "Cala Pura", called up captain, gave us weather forecast, 25-30 knots wind in Caribbean. All good so far today, sea and wind going our way.

Got days wrong, thought Sam's PhD result was tomorrow, and while sending her a satellite text to wish her good luck, She replied to say it was today! And I could now call her Dr. Gardner!! Fantastic !! (Red Coat Blog).

Position: 17' 04.375" N, 53' 28.024" W.   1854.   17/01/08

The Doctor Sam quote of the day, "You've got to ask yourself one question... do I feel lucky? Well do ya, punk?"

Friday 18th January 2008

Notebook/log only: Weather gone crazy, totally against all forecasts, including the "Cala Pura" one! Met tanker no. 10 "Santiago Express" didn't call up, it just went well past.

Position: 17' 02.661" N, 54' 22.290" W.   1831.   18/01/08.

The Sam quote of the day, "It's 106 miles to Chicago, we've got a full tank of gas, half a packet of cigarettes, it's dark and we're wearing sunglasses ... hit it!"

Saturday 19th January 2008

Notebook/log only: Texts from home to ring "Go Commando" who are apparently very close. Their position beacon has been on the blink for a while so no idea where they are exactly, but no amount of texting or Radio calls contact them, all quiet. Second visit from Stu on "Sara" very welcome but unexpected, he gave us instructions for the Antigua approach, which gave us a funny shiver. We have to ring ABSAR (Antigua and Barbuda Search And Rescue), at 20 n/miles, call duty officer, keep VHF radio on, then call them again at 5 n/miles. Stu had heard my talk with "Cala Pura" on the radio the other night. Had first real sighting of a proper Frigate Bird, bloody great thing just like a Pterodactyl, frightened me! Stu warned of bad weather imminent, which arrived after dark...very rough. We rigged up hand steering, which is great as long as wind going right way!!

Position: 17' 00.417! N, 54' 31.770" W.   12 noon. 19/01/08.

Sunday 20th January 2008 (by Jen)

No updated blog yet from Steve, but received a photo from Becs his daughter, showing him having his head shaved before leaving Cornwall back last November.

 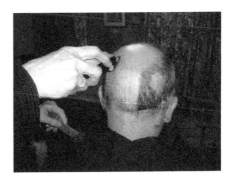

The Gardner family, apart from Baggins the dog, leave Zennor tonight to make the long journey to Antigua. Arrival date for Steve and Paul aboard "The Reason Why" is estimated at being in about one week's time.

Notebook/log: Remarkably hand steering got us nearly 50 miles when added to earlier. 354 miles to go at 8am but very big rough sea. Arse is shot. Constant squalls and heavy rain showers, now becoming very unpleasant.

Position: 16' 59.787" N, 55' 45.048" W. 1302. 20/01/08

Rained all day on and off, hand steered, it was brilliant not having to sit on that rowing seat, and still making ground. 12 noon and we'd been 7 weeks...49 days, at sea in this boat...unbelievable!

The Gus washed overboard incident/Adventure!!! full onward through the night. The Grinning Turk came out, but was threatened with cloud.

Position (2): 16' 58.634" N, 56' 04.042 W. 2100. 20/01/08.

The Sam quote of the day, "I don't believe in germs. Germs is just a plot they made up so they can sell you disinfectants and soaps!" "Now he's crazy, right?" "See? Ah! Ah! There's no right, there's no wrong there's only popular opinion."

Monday 21st January 2008

We were being pounded by huge waves coming over the aft cabin hatch, and at times, great "fizzers" would smack the sides of "The Reason Why", or fizz down the gunnels and dissolve into the foam some way in front. (we called them fizzers, because at night, even though you couldn't see them, you could hear them as they approached and hit, or slid past, and they made a fizzing noise as they moved. They did the same in the daylight, but you could see them coming!) When they hit, they sent a wall of white foam over us. In fact, we think our nicknames should be "squalls" because we must have had every squall in the Atlantic come down on us yesterday and last night. You could see them coming in waves, some would miss you and pass in front, others behind, but now and again you saw the one, and knew it was going to get you. The wind that came before the rain was good though, as it was like getting a very strong push and rowing became easier and speed increased markedly. But then the rain caught up and pounded the sea flat, bouncing up a foot or so and forming a weird mist that hovered just above the surface of the water. We just pulled over our hoods, looked down and let it pass, you couldn't do much in that!

Anyway, poor Gus the Black Bag Gorilla, was having to hang on for dear life to the cable ties that he was attached to, on the rail on top of the aft cabin. We'd heard him swearing and cursing under his breath, in his true mid-Atlantic gibberish, when suddenly, an enormous wave crashed over us, soaking us yet again. When we went to put the debris, usually Go bar wrappers and crisp bags, into Gus, to our horror...he wasn't there! For a moment we were distraught, until looking behind us, there he was...sitting there in the middle of the boat...grinning as cool as you like. How wind and wave had contrived to rip Gus off the aft cabin and overboard, only to deposit him once more back on board, albeit amidships, is a mystery. But there you are... Gus's little adventure ... and a true story too!

Droops (the watchpig) is sunburnt, I'm afraid, but still has the coolest oink and is still attached to the top of the aft cabin, next to Gus, and tied on with a binder twine life line!

We did see a frigate bird both yesterday and today, ruddy great pterodactyl, She was called Freda!

We have had a second visit from Stu in "Sara", and I don't think he could believe what he saw ... a rowing boat moving like a buttered pig towards Antigua, manned only by two old gits with a combined age of 97 ... but then neither can we!

Well done to Pura Vida, we still wear your wristbands, and as true supporters, may well claim a pint when we make land, hopefully at the weekend. Seriously lads, very well done!

The box that charges the laptop has just blown up, so this may be the last blog until we make land and it's all over – we'll have to see how the battery lasts.

(at this point, I did put my "prayer to Mo"...I've no idea why, but now I have put it where I should have in the first place ... at the start of the row).

Oblution notes:- some weeks ago we felt that the water maker wouldn't let us down, so we spared some fresh water and had washing days for towels and clothes, but the salt wind dried then clean but crispy! We treat cleaning our teeth as a pleasure to look forward to, as it is a bit of a performance, but we make a good job of it every few days, whether we need to or not! Paul brought a portable solar shower, the first time we took it out of storage to set up, a wave came and washed it overboard! We never even took it out of its box!

So that's it, still some rowing to do as we head for the 250 n/miles to go mark. Our families are arriving in Antigua, and we can't wait to see them, and our fellow rowers. Thank you again for the endless messages of support, and for all the monetary donations to our charity, Cornwall Hospice Care. Hope to see most of you soon. Love Steve and Paul.

This is a "fizzer"

Notebook/log: Chris and family flew to Antigua today!

299 miles to go at 12 noon. Good luck and Gods speed to all crews. Pura Vida well done, and No Fear... you'll have to lead the singing on "Trelawny" now!!! Well done Bill and Peter in Gquama, and well done Ben and Orlando in "Go Commando", whether you beat us or no – see you for a pint drekkly! Two more Pilot whales turned up briefly.

Position: 16' 57.164" N, 56' 51.680" W.   1955.   21/01/08.

The Sam quote of the day, "I can do anything... I'm the chief of police!"

For more than three weeks now, we have been trying to stay on 17', which takes us pretty much straight into Antigua, and I can't begin to tell you how tricky, that seemingly simple task is. Every day the wind or the sea, or both, try to drive us south down into the 16', or north up above 17'. We have just about managed it, a few minutes either way, but it has not been as easy as it may look!

Tuesday 22nd January 2008

Notebook/log only: Passed 250 miles to go at 8am. Closest tanker yet, no.11. Spoke to a not too friendly captain, very big, very close (a few hundred yards) "Burlington" something or other it was called, glad to see it pass by!! Good night on oars, passed 200 miles to go. The Sam quote of the day, "Hey Derice! Ya dead?" "No Mon, I'm not dead, but I have to finish the race!"

The Rum Has Gone

In the early morn as the sun comes up

And coffee fills up the breakfast cup

The brightest start cannot hide the con...

For dark is the night when the rum has gone.

The midday heat is hard to bear

Beneath The Sun's relentless glare

But there's no relief as the day moves on...

For dark is the night when the rum has gone.

Evening time follows afternoon

The day's design full circle soon

But the unknown author signs anon...

For dark is the night when the rum has gone.

It's six o'clock and The Sun sinks low

Sundowner time in the golden glow

But tonight there's shadow where once it shone...

For dark is the night when the rum has gone.

Sg2008

Wednesday 23rd January 2008

Notebook/log only: Sat phone playing up, receiving some texts, but not sure if ours are getting back. All a bit anxious here, knowing families await in Antigua, and the sea is frustratingly turning to treacle more often than not, and seemingly putting up a hell of a fight to try and delay us. Rowing hard, sometimes 2 up to try and keep near the schedule. "Unfinished Business" became "Finished" today, well done girls.

No more e-mailed blogs until Antigua I'm afraid, plug got wet and blew up, everything is wet to be honest.

Passed the 180 miles to go point, which is where Chris Barrett and Bob Warren in "Spirit of Cornwall" came to grief 2 years ago. We stopped briefly and toasted their health with port (the rum having gone...I may have mentioned it, and the Southern Comfort is for first sight of land). "There but for the grace of God, go I" we said, sipping our port.

The Sam quote of the day, "I've had it! If anyone sees me go near a boat again they have my permission to shoot me!"

With the excitement and anticipation, tinged with just a tad of desperation, I hardly wrote a thing in the notebook for the 24th or 25th January. I didn't even update the positions, and of course the laptop was out of action.

The Sam quote of the day still got through, "Louis, I think this is the beginning of a beautiful friendship." This could have been the 24th January.

Last page of the notebook/log read, "Passed 100 to go in the night. Arrival should be Saturday late pm. Friday night doubled up 70 – 54 miles to go. Passed out...over did it? Paul hurt his hip...woke up at 49 miles to go."

The Sam quote of the day, "Worth waiting for!" was on 25th. I think?

Then there was a scribble, "large pod of dolphins following us 30+. 3 knots all day...

The famous red coat with beard!

Tanker no 9 - "Cala Pura"

We had doubled up rowing overnight, and with us both rowing, and with help from the wind and waves at last, we had knocked seventeen miles off the slowly, but ever decreasing total of nautical miles to the finish line. Mind you, we had really pushed it, and had taken no rest between our individual rows and doubling up, but we were being driven by the overwhelming desire to meet up with friends and families that we knew were already in Antigua, and had been, for more than four days waiting for us. It was also Saturday, and whilst just two days previous, we had hoped to arrive in the early hours of Monday morning, or at best late Sunday night, we suddenly saw a chance by hard work and a fair wind, of arriving in the early hours of Sunday morning, or better still… late Saturday night!

But as usual, just as we thought we were away, everything was going for us and Mo had given in and was going to allow us to cross, a wave smacked into the side of the boat in the dark, we didn't see or hear it coming, and we were mid change over, putting the rig back for one person rowing once more. It caught us both off balance, and sent Paul flying forward, his hip crashing into the metal end of the seat runners in the middle of the boat, and he let out a groan of pain, and I knew straight away it must have hurt him.

I had been knocked backwards towards the aft cabin hatch, and had collapsed in a heap on the seat over the water maker, not sure what I hit, but I don't remember anything hurting particularly. But as I tried to sit up to see how Paul was, who was rubbing his hip and trying to see if there was any visible damage, I felt myself falling … falling in slow motion, over and over again, and everything went black, except for the stars … swirling, flashing stars and streaks of light…… where was I? … What had happened?

For some reason I was doubled over, my head falling lower and lower, almost into Paul's lap, and I sort of knew it was happening but could do nothing about it. Paul suddenly noticed me, and immediately thought I was messing about … but I wasn't. I heard him call me …

"Steve! … what are you doing?" But I couldn't see him … I couldn't see anything except swirling lights. I struggled to sit up, straining to see something … anything, but I couldn't get my eyes to see through the flashing stars and lights that seemed to be swirling in black treacle. It was quite scary for a moment or two, but slowly things started to clear … I started to recognize things again … I looked down the boat, that was coming back into focus, and back at Paul, who was sitting there looking at me …

"I thought you were messing about" he said

"No, must have blacked out for a minute" I said

"We've been pushing hard tonight, doubling up like that on top of our individual rowing, we've had no rest for the night, and... we haven't eaten anything, not enough anyway" Paul continued

I could do with a lie down a minute, how are you?" I said

"Bruised my hip, but its ok," he said, "I'll just keep dabbling us along so we're moving forward, we're ok"

"I'll just lie down a minute, won't be long" I said gingerly crawling through the hatch.

When I woke up about an hour later, I think, I felt fine, and climbed out of the cabin, and glanced at the GPS, and had to look twice, as it said 46 nautical miles to go. "Is that right?" I said, now fully out of the cabin and stretching upright. I gave Droops a squeeze, and he gave me a reassuring if slightly hoarse "oink!"

"Yep ... that's right, last night bought us half a day ... you alright now?" said Paul

"Yeh ... just must have overdone it ... have a rest, I'll take over and have a go for a while now ... look at the "Go Bar" wrappers ... how many have you had?" I said

"Only 2 or 3 ... or so" he said a little sheepishly. I stood gazing into the west ... into the still very dark night, The Grinning Turk being nowhere about as usual, "It's fifty miles away, you won't see it yet" continued Paul. "Forty-six, and I'm going to look anyway!" I replied. "That's nautical miles, you can't see that far ... and it's still dark!" came back Paul

"They have lights don't they ... in Antigua, and what about the lighthouse, we ought to see that a long way off ..." I said, "Not this far" said Paul, "We're not there yet! "Well" said Paul, "Can you see anything?"... "No!" I said sharply.

We changed over and decided to keep to an hour on and an hour off, from now on. And in this way, soon, the first pale light of dawn crept up over the Eastern horizon, banishing the unseen terrors of the night, and putting in their place a beacon of warmth, light and hope, that sent a flicker of excitement through our bodies, and for the very first time we dared to believe. We were on the edge of something special ... we felt it bubbling to the surface ... something that we had dare not think of, but kept locked deep in our inner most dreams...

At the end of every hour, we would stare into the West, for that first glimpse of our goal ... our paradise island ... and land.

The mileage entered the thirties, and it was daylight, but quite hazy, not helping our eager eyes at all. "I'm going to look" said Paul, towards the end of his rest hour, and he stood up and looked over my head into the West. "Too hazy" I said, "...and too far". "I'm going to look anyway ... you looked hours ago ... in the dark!" said Paul. There was a pause as Paul peered westward into the haze. "Well ... can you see it?" I said. "No!" was the sharp reply.

And so it continued all morning, but the mood had changed. The past few days had pushed us to the limit in our desperate attempts to get to our families and that finish line. With no definite end or timescale to depend upon, and with the ocean turning to treacle on increasingly regular occasions, we both felt that the end of our time on the boat, fantastic as She had been, was now overdue. But on this morning, the tension had gone, the spring had unwound, and had been replaced with an undercurrent of excitement, bubbling just under the surface, and it only needed the merest twist of a thin wire, to un pop the cork holding back a river of joy.

The air of excitement and anticipation grew as the morning went on, but we made a point of continually looking back East until changeover, so we had a full hours travel West, between looks, giving us the best chance of a dramatically different horizon. But each time, the expectation as we turned to look, sank almost immediately, as once again there was only sea, sky and that haze.

The breeze suddenly picked up, blowing from the East, helping us on our way, as if a giant will had finally given in, and let us go from its, or her, clutches. With wind and sea behind us, we were effortlessly making 3 – 3.5 knots, and the mood had become positively lighthearted, and with the breeze, the haze began to clear and the sun shone brightly down on us, as if to suit our mood.

As lunchtime approached, I jumped up for changeover, and turned to look over Paul and the bow of the boat … almost automatically showing the disappointment I had experienced every other time I had looked so far … just the usual I thought, as I looked down to find my trainers, but something made me look up again … I strained and screwed up my eyes. What was I looking at? Was it a shadow … far away, faint and on the edge of sight, almost imperceptible in the rapidly clearing haze … a slightly darker outline. Was it there, or was I seeing things?

Three seconds later I yelled, "LAND!!! I CAN SEE IT!!! THERE IT IS!!!"

Paul jumped and stopped rowing to turn and look where I pointed over his shoulder.

The GPS said 26.2 nautical miles, and there, after 3000 miles and 55 days of nothing but the empty wastes of The Atlantic Ocean, we were going to make it, even if we had to swim towing the boat behind us, we were going to make it, for there … directly in front of us … was land … Antigua … paradise found … and our lives would never be the same again.

Saturday 26th January 2008 (by Jen)

Well today is hopefully the last day for Paul and Steve on board The Reason Why. It is anticipated that they should make landfall about midnight tonight, giving them a race time of around 55 days. The plan was always to try and take between 50 and 60 days, so they are bang on the middle of their target. As soon as I hear of their arrival, I will publish the official time here, although if you, like me are looking at the ARR website several times a day, having nothing else to do!!?? Ha ha, it will no doubt be on there as well. I expect there will be a party organised when the return to Cornwall, and any details of that will appear here too.

In the meantime, enjoy the last day of the row for Paul and Steve. Steve will no doubt update the blog as soon he has had a few beers, and has recovered from spending 55 days on "The Reason Why" with Paul, Mo, Gus, Droops and The Grinning Turk!!

Message received at 01.50pm GMT - land has been spotted by Paul and Steve, with under 27 miles left to row. Two very happy rowers!

Phone call received at 08.45pm GMT – all well aboard "The Reason Why" with only 8 miles left to row. Paul phoned to give me an update whilst Steve was busy rowing, but he still managed to shout out some bits and pieces! They are currently moving at approximately 3 knots, so expect to cross the finish line about midnight here, which is of course only 8pm in Antigua! Their bums are very sore and their hands are in a claw like state, but other than that they are fine. Pauls's knee has been no problem, as has Steve's back. They have both lost weight, and recently Steve got out his shorts that he hadn't worn since La Gomera, and Paul reckons there's room in them for both rowers!!

Once they Cross the finish line, they will be met by The Antigua and Barbuda Search And Rescue (ABSAR), who will confirm the official time with Woodvale and let me now. Paul has promised to send some photos through, but until we hear of the finish, that's all there is for now, but will keep everyone posted with news, as and when I get any.

Notebook/log: ... Mo has given in, wind and sea helping us, and at this rate will be in for a few beers tonight. **LAND HO** .... 26.2 Miles on **GPS**.

Finished English Harbour, Antigua 8.03pm local time, 26/01/08 (0003 UK time)

Time 55 days 12 hours 3 minutes

(Sam's final quote, has me in tears every time, by the way...)

The Sam final quote of the day, "Here at last, on the shores of the sea, comes the end of our fellowship. I will not say do not weep ... for not all tears are an evil"

First contact, Antigua; dolphins follow us in; local fishermen pay us a call

I could smell land, long before Pinky and Perky here could see it! As we got closer I saw the approaching game fishing boats, long before them as well. In fact one of them came very close, and shouted over saying that they had tracked a Sailfish for some while, and it was now right under The Reason Why! But despite looking all round, we couldn't see anything, and very soon, they shouted their farewells and went speeding off again, in search of Marlin and further Sailfish. Then came the smaller, local fishermen, in their distinctively Caribbean boats, a couple of which were only metres away when Paul and Steve saw them, in fact they jumped...both times, as other voices became clear after so long in silence, apart from "MA" and their own voices of course. The fishermen chugged along with us for quite some time laughing and pointing, not quite sure about us, who we were , where we were going, and most probably what we were and where the hell had we come from?

As we got closer to land, the air was different ... the sea was different ... the light was different. Frigate birds hung in the air like latter day pterodactyls, with their enormous wingspans hinged in the same way as their prehistoric forbears, looking for fish. After everything, it was a great last day, sunny and hot, the wind and sea were with us, and the demons of the last few days were forgotten, banished to the landless wastes of the mighty ocean behind us.

I saw the school of dolphins break the surface behind us, playing in the surf , arching out of the water then disappearing back under the waves, at least twenty or thirty,(I like to believe there was forty-two ... it just had to be didn't it?)

When Steve and Paul first spotted land, did they hurry towards it... no! They stopped rowing and sat drinking ... just staring at it, as if *it*, was coming to them! I oinked in annoyance, oops...I suddenly realise that nobody had squeezed me, but they didn't even notice, knocking back the Southern Comfort miniatures saved from that Christmas thing. So I oinked again, in defiance, silently screaming "get me off this oinking boat!"

Eventually they rowed on, and now, the shadow on the horizon that they said was Antigua, got rapidly nearer and larger, and as it began to get dark it filled the horizon. Lights appeared on the shore, and on boats that seemed to be coming out to meet us.

They had called A.B.S.A.R. (Antigua and Barbuda Search And Rescue), at 20 miles and again at 5 miles, as instructed and we had heard "Go Commando" do the same three hours or so earlier, and it would seem they were going to pip us to the post...just, after all.

It was then the dozy prats decided to ignore the GPS. This is the same GPS that had successfully navigated them across three thousand miles of the empty tracts of The Atlantic Ocean, and hit Antigua right on the button, and they ignored it, deciding to head by line of sight to the headland they could see in front of them, which was obviously the correct one!

Unfortunately it was not, and in any case, the other obvious flaw in the plan, was that they couldn't see even the wrong headland in the dark!

Luckily they realised this before they'd gone too far wrong, about a mile, and headed back in, and back on course.

I could sense the excitement as they coordinated positions on the radio with the rapidly approaching boats, hearing familiar voices, I could feel their emotions, and began to feel not unemotional myself. It seemed to be Stu, on board "Sara", loaded with their families and a second yacht we didn't know, named "Windsong" with more family and anyone who couldn't get on "Sara". Voices calling in the dark from both yachts either side, voices from unseen bodies in the night, "Well Done Dad!"; "Hey Paul" ; "Hey Steve". They called back and began to identify where wives, sons and daughters all were, and you could physically feel the electricity crackling and the pride bristling between the two yachts, with "The Reason Why" in between them, and even I, pink plastic pig ... that's Watchpig to you ... felt the lump of emotion in my throat.

The A.B.S.A.R rib appeared with Amanda on board with the search and rescue guys, and a finishing klaxon. We were apparently still at too sharp an angle to the land and had a little row still to the finish line, so they rowed for what seemed like ages, but was probably about half an hour, right up to, and nearly under the cliff, the A.B.S.A.R. chap telling us it was deep water all the way in so don't worry about the proximity of the cliff. The rib then roared off ahead, and still they rowed, and both began to say, "where the hell is this finish line?" Finally, looking ahead, I could see the rib, stationary, about fifty yards ahead, Paul and Steve saw it too, and concentrated on their timing, and rowed hard for the line. The yachts cleared out of the way, and renewed shouts of encouragement echoed under the cliff. They pulled up to the rib... nothing, they pulled seemingly past the rib ... nothing, then finally the line was crossed and the wailing, slightly eerie but wonderful klaxon sounded, signalling the end of the race. The Atlantic Ocean was crossed, it was a defining moment none of us, would ever forget.

The lump in my throat grew somewhat, making a celebratory oink out of the question. I looked down at the two blokes who had mercilessly stuck me to the cabin roof, and rowed me across The Atlantic, they had now stopped rowing and had turned to face each other, hands outstretched, clasped in a firm shake, as they looked straight at each other, and said, "well done mate" and "we did it", and after a reflective pause of satisfaction, soaking up the moment, "let's get her in!" as if they'd just finished a gig race, and at that moment, the enormity of what they had done ... nay, what we had done, hit me.

All acrimony or ill will I had felt towards these people disappeared in that moment, and the lump in my throat rose higher up my head, and emerged through one of my eyes as a tear. "Wow," I thought, I didn't expect that.

It had all gone quiet, "The Reason Why" was on its own again, the silence now felt strange after the noise of the last hour or so, for the yachts had motored off to

English Harbour, maybe five hundred yards further on, past Cape Shirley, which was where we were at present. The rib had gone ahead too, and it was odd to be alone again, but up ahead, "Sara" was waiting, with a light, at the entrance to English Harbour, making sure we didn't miss it in the dark, as it wasn't obvious, and sailed off to moor up and unload passengers ashore, only as we approached them, and they were sure we knew where to go.

As we got to where "Sara" had been, Paul and Steve rowed into the dark space between the cliffs, beneath a ruined fort up on the point, guarding the entrance to English Harbour, which suddenly and spontaneously burst into life, making us all jump, with screaming, yelling banshees, letting off and waving, red, white and orange smoke flares, klaxons, sirens and air horns and manual hooters being pushed to lips and blown wildly. The noise and the smoke was so surprising and utterly overwhelming, given the past 55 days of solitude, and another tear followed the first. Was this all for them ... for us?

There was definitely Robbie from "Pura Vida", Joe, Tara and Emily from "Unfinished Business" and a few others I couldn't see in the shadows, but from the noise and smoke they made there could have been fifty people in that fort, that had been one minute a black empty ruin, and the next a fiery cauldron of noise and light. We were drifting, just staring, not able to take it all in. The radio crackled into life, it was the A.B.S.A.R. rib, "This way ... "Reason Why" ... look for my light, you must come away from there, you're drifting under the fort and you're nearly on the rocks!"

Blimey, that would be ideal, three thousand miles across The Atlantic, and we get wrecked on the rocks of English Harbour, but Steve and Paul seemed to snap out of their wide eyed trance that they slipped into as soon as the flares went up, and gripping the oars, slowly rowed round, away from the rocks, and over towards the light on the A.B.S.A.R. rib some 150 yards away. They still looked stunned and amazed, we all were, gobsmacked would be a good description, and as we made our way, very slowly, through the maze of moored yachts throughout the harbour, we realised that most of them had people on them, cheering and clapping, shouting their congratulations, letting off air horns and hooters, lighting flares and raising glasses. This was a welcome unexpected, surpassing our wildest dreams or imaginings, in truth, I hadn't imagined this moment at all, and looking at Steve and Paul ... neither had they, but I know it will be something all of us remember for the rest of our lives.

Suddenly, we slid clear of the yachts and moorings, and across a short space of still, perfectly glassy water. We saw the quay of Nelson's Dockyard, illuminated by yet more flares and smoke, more air horns and hooters, and the red flares and smoke reflected off the mirror like water and gave the whole scene a wonderful red glow. The quay was awash with more people, maybe eighty to a hundred lining the whole length of the quay we were slowly but surely approaching. Looking to the right, we could see the lights of flares flickering through the trees, being held by people running along the track from the fort on the head, where we had first been greeted, at the entrance to English Harbour, the air horns and klaxons sounding, as if war had broken out.

As we slowly floated up to the quay, more cheering and applause, hooters and smoke, we all thought there must be someone else arriving, someone famous, The Queen of Sheba was the first thought! But no, there were the families all dressed in the blue "Reason Why" t-shirts, clapping and cheering, cameras clicking. Just metres from the wall I saw Steve getting a little fractious as the gate holding the bow oar would not unscrew, it had seized up with the salt water, and any second the boat was going to hit the quay and snap the oar. In the nick of time, Steve got it loose, and lifted out the oar as the last two meters disappeared and saw the boat come along side the quay, Paul having been seemingly unaware of the problem.

Steve was standing near the bow as we came alongside, and handed the bow rope to Carl from "Pura Vida", sporting his "Reason Why" t-shirt, who was nearest, with Nick from "No Fear", and before he knew it, Carl and Nick had grabbed Steve's arm to help him ashore, almost before he was ready, none of us having set foot on land for more than 55 days, but one step up, and further helped by Amanda from Woodvale, and Steve was ashore, Carl, Nick and Amanda steadying him as he was mobbed by his family, wife Chris, daughters Sam and Rebecca, son Oliver, and future son in law, Alex. At the stern of the boat, Paul did the same, and stepped ashore, and was steadied by wife Dawn, Robbie from "Pura Vida" and Ben from "Go Commando", before hugging his wife, son Jake and daughter Danielle.

It was about now that I felt a very strange and unexpected sensation ... it was over ...they, we had done it ... and I suddenly didn't want to leave, or want it to be over ... another tear fell.

There were so many greetings, and hugs and kisses, Steve and Paul stumbled about like drunken sailors, their legs not coping well, if at all, with the strange sensation of stillness and the permanence of dry land. They were passed from person to person, all wanting a hug. After their families, several times, came the other rowers, Carl and Robbie from "Pura Vida", Nick from "No Fear", Jo Tara and Emily from "Unfinished Business", Ben and Orlando from "Go Commando", (who, incidentally, I found out later only beat us, after 55 days of racing, by 3 hours and 26 minutes!!), and of course Amanda from Woodvale, who proceeded to make Steve and Paul kneel down for a photo ... I didn't think they'd get up again to be honest. I saw Oliver pass his Dad his first beer in nearly two months, for which Oliver got a big pat on the back, and a "that's my boy!" I saw Sam and Rebecca, Steve's daughters, looking so alike with their big brown eyes and long dark hair, Paul with Jake and Danielle, Dawn and Chris trying to keep their husbands from falling over, and I saw a thousand Kodak moments, photograph after photograph, and the air fair bristled with pride and joy.

Amanda started the scrutineering that had to be done there and then, checking we still had all the mandatory equipment and were "up to weight", most important was the emergency water/ballast, and that it was still there, all intact and untouched since Amanda sealed the 5 litre containers, two months ago in La Gomera. We knew of course, that it was, as our water maker had performed brilliantly, keeping us topped up in fresh water every time it was asked.

Steve and Paul were not much help in this, staggering about, deliriously happy, and Sam, Alex, Rebecca and Oliver, helped Nick unpack the boat, and pile equipment and the thirty, 5 litre water containers out on the quay. Gus was taken, stuffed full of food wrappers and all the packaging and rubbish that had to be brought back with us, I hardly had time to say goodbye to Gus. All checked, counted, inspected and passed, including anchor and chain, we were declared legal and within the rules by Amanda, and talk began of going to the nearest bar, which apparently was on the back of the quay. Steve was quite keen to see if they had the rum!

Suddenly, Steve took everyone by surprise, much to the horror of his family, by stepping back on board "The Reason Why", as they were sure he'd fall in, both him and Paul were still very unsteady on their legs. But they need not have worried, back on the boat, Steve was sure footed again, with water under him, as he searched "The Bear Pit" for the clean shirt he'd been saving for this moment.

As he joked around with his elf ears hat on, posing for more photographs, he turned and looked at me, and said, "well done Droops!" and gave me a squeeze. I was so shocked, and touched, that no oink came out, and he had to squeeze me again, before I managed a fairly feeble but emotional, deeply felt and appreciative oink!

Soon enough, everyone was drifting off to "The Galley Bar", and suddenly it was quiet once again. There on my own, I thought, "That has got to be the best moment of my life!" just being a part of this.

A smile passed my lips and stuck on my slightly faded, pink plastic face, and a tear trickled silently down my badly faded snout, as a long satisfied oink of contentment came from somewhere deep within me ... but nobody heard ... and there was nobody there to see.

The reception committee, our families waiting to hear...and the last few strokes

This was the nearest photo to us crossing the line, 2003 local time, Sat.26/01/2008.

154

The fort at the entrance to English Harbour looked a dark ruin one minute...before all hell let loose the next! We were spell bound and nearly went aground on the rocks beneath the fort. It is actually called Fort Berkeley, we found out later.

From the wild, bright noisy welcome of the fort, more of the same was to follow as we came through the moored yachts up to the quay in Nelson's Dockyard.

Nelson's Dockyard after the smoke... and then the first steps ashore...

A thousand Kodak moments...

We staggered about like drunken sailors, in seventh heaven.

Amanda wanted us to kneel down, Droops thought we'd never get up (so did I!)

Official welcome from Antigua and Barbuda Tourist Board, a bag of goodies each

Back - Carl, Robbie, "Us", Joe, Emily, Nick front - Ben, Orlando, Tara.

The Gardner's... Alex, Sam, Yours truly, Chris, Oliver, Rebecca.

The Harris's... Dawn, Paul, Danielle, Jake.

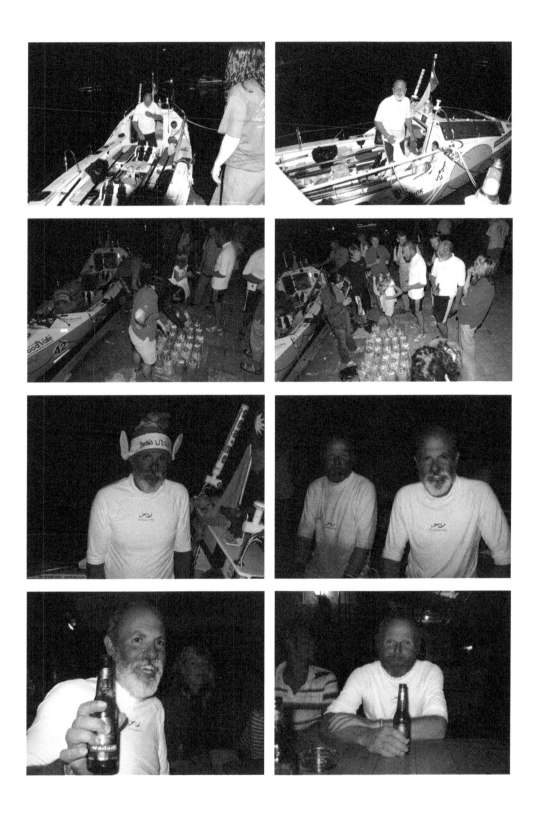

Thank You Prayer To Mo

Mighty Ocean here we stand

You let us pass from Land to Land

We saw your endless beauty free

Your awesome power and majesty

No win or lose for you or us

The Reason Why or Droops or Gus

For fifty days and five as one

Together till our journey done

Mighty Mo you're still the boss

But thanks to you we're safe across.

sg2008

Saturday 26th January 2008 (written in Antigua on 29th Jan)

So here we are, two men, one boat, and two buckets (actually three...we had a spare!), Droops has clocked off as Watch Pig, and Gus has said his last goodbye's and gone off to do greater things and line greater bins!

Antigua ... wow! We first saw it 26.2 miles out and frantically worked out whether we could get in by closing time! We had doubled up rowing the night before, to try and pull Antigua within a day's row, fifty miles ish. We didn't know we were going to get a 3 knot helping wind all the next day, Saturday, which improved our E.T.A. in Antigua by two hours, plus we still had our joker to play. We were still on Reason Why time, which was two hours ahead of Antigua! Suddenly, we were not only going to make Saturday, we were going to get a Saturday night out to boot!

We spoke to A.B.S.A.R. (The Antigua and Barbuda Search And Rescue), and Woodvale at 20 miles and 5 miles as instructed, and we were met by support yacht "Sara" and a second yacht, "Windsong" whose Captain was a mate of Nick's from "No Fear" and he agreed to go out with "Sara" and meet us, with our families on board, spread over the two yachts. So thanks to Nick and "Windsong" for that. The A.B.S.A.R. rib was there too, with Amanda and the finishing klaxon.

Once across the line, which was far from easy, we received the most incredible and completely unforgettable welcome. As we rowed into English Harbour, suddenly the inky black night (no sign of the Turk as usual), burst into light from all the rowers who had already arrived, leaping up on the ramparts of the old fort at the entrance to the harbour, waving orange and red smoke flares. Air horns deafened us and echoed all around the whole of English Harbour. Every moored yacht also burst into life, with horns and lights and shouts of welcome. The "Pura Vida" boys, the "Unfinished Business" girls, (now "Finished Business"), the "No Fear" boys and even those pesky "Commando's" were there to welcome us, and caused most of the smoke and noise! As we came up to dock, there seemed to be hundreds of people cheering and shouting and handing out bottles of beer and bacon rolls, families all together again, those long awaited hugs, and a welcome committee from The Antigua and Barbuda Tourist Board, and a dozen photo calls, well, I suppose it was a Kodak moment. I have to say that we were totally overwhelmed, and it has to be one of the most special and memorable moments of my life, we will never forget it. Difficult to stand up, we wobbled like drunken sailors and proceeded with everyone else, without so much as a shower, to "The Galley Bar", until 1.30am. It was simply perfect, and had to be done ... and done right!

We achieved a crossing time of 55 days 12 hours and 3 minutes, arriving across the finishing line in Antigua, at 8.03 pm. and guess what ... they even had the rum!

Finally, we have a holiday to enjoy with our families now, for a week or so, and thank goodness the fear of not getting to Antigua in time, proved unfounded. On top of everything else, it turns out that "The Reason Why" has completed the 200th successful ocean crossing ever, and they made quite a fuss of us about this. We may get a certificate or something, apparently, and this has very definitely put the icing on what was already a memorable and incredible journey.

Thanks for the support from so many, especially our families, Droops, Gus; Amanda, Tony and Simon from Woodvale; A.B.S.A.R; Stu, Andrea and John on "Sara"; and of course a very special thanks to Jen, the third member of "The Reason Why" team back home in Cornwall, who has of course been the person responsible for the website and publishing the blog and the photos etc. of not just the row, but the whole adventure, going back nearly 2 years, as well as keeping us informed during the row nearly 24 hours a day. THANKS JEN.

Tuesday 29th January 2008

Simon Chalk and his 5 man boat "Oyster Shack" (it was a 6 man boat, but someone got injured, at the last minute, so they decided to go as a 5, which was a good move as it happens, as they narrowly missed the 6 man record, 35 days and some, but their time of 37 days and some, holds the never attempted before 5 man record!), so there will be much rejoicing tonight, I expect in the marvellous "Mad Mongoose" bar. "Pendovey Swift" is expected later in the week, so we look forward to greeting Joss and Ian... he won the London River Race you know! Then it looks like "Komale" at the weekend or just past. Touch and go whether we are still here. This is Niall and James, who had special permission to leave a couple of days after the rest of us from La Gomera, because of Niall's poisoned arm, that the doctor said wasn't ready to be rowed with on 2nd December.

You might like to know that although the official distance from La Gomera to Antigua is 2552 nautical miles, (2931 miles), our GPS tells us that we have actually rowed, because of wind and waves, nearer 3000 nautical miles, (3400miles)!!

Thanks again for showing us so much support, and so much interest in our blog, I may have to put it all in a book, I've had so many requests to do so. Please keep the donations coming in – Cornwall Hospice Care needs your support too.

I thought you may like to know, those who have been following the blog, that the view from our hotel window, is a six foot fence, in front of which lies three chunks of concrete rubble, an old coil of water pipe, a rusting step ladder, and yes ... both a scabby dog and a scabby cat (well, they're not really scabby), and not a sign of the sea anywhere ... bloody perfect!!!

That's it Jen, see you next week

Love Steve x

P.S. Incidentally, any publishers interested in "The Reason Why – The Book of The Blog" ... we're open to offers!

Now I suppose I can't finish without a poem, I will write a thank you prayer to "Mo" at some point whilst over here, but for now, this will have to do ...

Our Journey's End

So here we are

Our journey's end

The Mighty Mo

Our new found friend

Three thousand miles

And maybe more

From Gomeran dock

To Antiguan shore.

Sometimes we stalled

When seas were big

At others moved

Like a buttered pig.

We kept our heads

When things looked glum

Like Wolf Fish stew

And the final rum.

We chased the wind

It chased us back

From Spanish Isle

To The Rastus Shack.

Those shooting stars

The night came soon

The Grinning Turk

Our part time moon.

Beneath the clouds

Beneath the Sun

The fizzing waves

That smack your bum

That Christmas came

And New Year went

The rum we had

Was heaven sent

And then the day

We saw the land

Emotions you can

Understand.

Then here we are

That welcome night

An English Harbour

Sheer delight

The lights and smoke

The klaxons sound

The rowers greet

Their Paradise found.

I won't forget

That welcome sight

Our families

The smoke and light.

The faces full

Of joy and cheer

The bacon rolls

And Wadadli beer.

Now like this row

The end has come

Farewell my friends

I'm off for rum!

sg2008

167

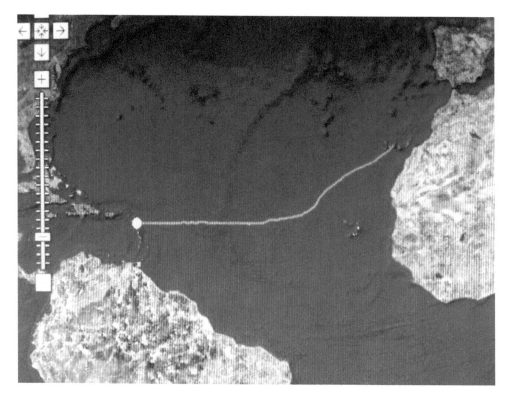

This was our course as recorded by the satellite tracking beacon on board. La Gomera being at the East (right) of the line, and Antigua the white dot to the West.

The Cornishman Newspaper – 7th February 2008

Zennor Gig Club rowers Steve Gardner and Paul Harris have joined an elite club of sportsmen after completing a mammoth 2936 mile charity race across The Atlantic. According to Steve, who at 51, was the oldest competitor to complete this year's race, more people have climbed Mount Everest and been into space than have rowed across an ocean. Supporters lined English Harbour in Antigua waving distress flares and sounding klaxons to guide the pair through the last few strokes of their gruelling journey. As they stepped on to dry land, they became the 200th crew ever to have successfully rowed across an ocean.

The two friends had set out in their 23 foot self built boat "The Reason Why" some 55 days, 12 hours and 3 minutes before, from La Gomera in The Canary Islands. Contract Manager Steve, said the trip had been "absolutely sensational" and declared that they had still not come down to earth. "We just hoped to finish, so to come in the first six overall, and fourth in the pairs class, is more than we could have dreamed of," he said, "There are crews of young fit guys out there, whose combined age doesn't add up to mine, who are still out on the ocean not finished the course yet." "Our calf muscles are screaming out as we haven't walked for nearly two months."

168

The duo followed in the footsteps of Olympic gold medallist James Cracknell, and TV presenter Ben Fogle, who competed in The Woodvale Atlantic Challenge two years ago, filming their progress for the BBC. The aim of Steve and Paul, is to raise up to £25,000 for Cornwall Hospice Care through sponsorship and the eventual sale of their state-of-the-art boat. The pair have already been contacted by potential buyers, but nothing has been decided yet.

Steve explained that the trip had contained a few "hairy" moments when their plywood craft came almost within "touching distance" of massive tankers and towering cruise ships. He said, "We had radar on board so we knew when large vessels were close, but some of them are a bit naughty, and don't turn their systems on, or have no-one on watch, so it's a bit frightening. It was spectacular at times too, with whales, pods of dolphins and schools of flying fish travelling through the air."

Steve, who lost two stones in weight during the voyage, said there had been a few difficult moments, particularly Christmas Day and New Year. "It is hard spending so much time together on a 23 foot boat, but we hardly had a cross word, and I think we got off the boat better friends than we got on."

Paul, who works as a technician for Western Power, said it felt strange to be back in Connor Downs and back at work. "It all seemed to go really quickly, looking back, as if it never happened." he said. The 46 year old, laughed off references to record breaking Olympian Steve Redgrave, who famously asked to be shot if he ever got back in a boat, and vowed not to undertake another ocean trip. "Well, there's an Indian Ocean race in 2009 but I am happy to go on record as saying, I will not be doing it."

Annie Binding, appeals manager for Cornwall Hospice Care, said, "It is an absolutely incredible feat, and I take my hat off to the pair of them. It's not just the rowing, but the amount of work they put in beforehand building the boat. The money raised is absolutely vital as we need £5 million each year just to continue our work. I'm hoping to see them both for a party, and buy the pair of them a beer to say thank you."

So that's it Blog readers, this was the final entry under "Race Blog" complete with "final poem" (page 158), well ... there may be one more.

Official Overall Race Placements for the Atlantic Rowing Race 2007

After 77 days at sea the final boat in the Atlantic Rowing Race 2007 crossed the line on Sunday 17th February. Packed full of excitement, anxiety, tension and joy (and that was just the spectators!) this years race has been one of the most exhilarating and closest races ever with all boats finishing within 29 days of each other.

Congratulations to everyone who took part in the race this year the camaraderie was second to none and the amount of support between teams overwhelming.

Thank you for making it such a race to remember and we hope, in fact we are certain, that lasting friendships have been made and memories have been created that will last a lifetime.

First Place:

Pura Vida crewed by Carl Theakston, Robbie Grant, John Cecil-Wright and Tom Harvey (UK)

Finished Saturday 19th January 14:52 GMT – crossing time 48 days, 2 hours and 5 minutes

Second Place:

Gquma Challenger crewed by Bill Godfrey and Peter Van Kets (South Africa)

Finished Tuesday 22nd January 00:15 GMT – crossing time 50 days, 12 hours and 15 minutes

Third Place:

No Fear crewed by Nick Histon and Jon Csehi (UK)

Finished Tuesday 22nd January 06:05 GMT – crossing time 50 days, 18 hours and 5 minutes

Fourth Place:

Unfinished Business crewed by Jo Davies, Tara Remington, Emily Kohl and Sarah Kessans (UK, New Zealand, USA)

Finished Wednesday 23rd January 04:31 GMT – crossing time 51 days, 16 hours and 31 minutes

Fifth Place:

Go Commando crewed by Orlando Rogers and Ben Gaffney (UK)

Finished Saturday 26th January 20:39 GMT – crossing time 55 days, 8 hours and 39 minutes

Sixth Place:

The Reason Why crewed by Steve Gardner and Paul Harris (UK)

Finished Sunday 27th January 00:03 GMT – crossing time 55 days, 12 hours and 3 minutes

Seventh Place:

Pendovey Swift crewed by Ian Andrews and Joss Elliot (UK)

Finished Sunday 3rd February 08:46 GMT – crossing time 62 days, 20 hours and 56 minutes

Eighth Place:

Komale crewed by James Burge and Niall McCann (UK)

Finished Tuesday 5th February 14:05 GMT – crossing time 63 days, 2 hours and 5 minutes (please note due to extenuating circumstances this team started 48 hours after the main racing fleet)

Ninth Place:

Jaydubyoo crewed by Andrew and Joe Jordon-White (UK)

Finished Thursday 7th February 07:43 GMT – crossing time 66 days, 19 hours and 43 minutes

Tenth Place:

Row of Life crewed by Angela Madsen and Franck Festor (USA, France)

Finished Thursday 7th February 11:24 GMT – crossing time 66 days, 23 hours and 24 minutes

Eleventh Place:

Ocean Summit crewed by Scott McNaughton and Neil Hunter (UK)

Finished Thursday 7th February 22:10 GMT – crossing time 67 days, 10 hours and 10 minutes

Twelfth Place:

Pygram crewed by Fabien Decourt and Benoit Dusser (France)

Finished Wednesday 13th February 15:03 GMT – crossing time 73 days, 3 hours and 3 minutes

Thirteenth Place:

Silver Cloud crewed by Fiona Waller, Sarah Duff, Clair Desborough and Rachel Flanders (UK)

Finished Thursday 14th February 13:03 GMT – crossing time 74 days, 1 hour and 3 minutes

Fourteenth Place:

1 Charmed Life crewed by Pete Collett (Australia)

Finished Saturday 16th February 11:46 GMT – crossing time 75 days, 23 hours and 46 minutes

Fifteenth Place:

C2 crewed by Ian McGlade and Andy Watson (Northern Ireland, UK)

Finished Wednesday 13th February 22:45 GMT – crossing time 73 days, 10 hours and 45 minutes (please note C2 lost two race placements due to using more than 110 litres of their total ballast water)

Sixteenth Place:

Spirit of Fernie crewed by Paul Attalla (Canada)

Finished Saturday 16th February 19:46 GMT – crossing time 76 days, 7 hours and 46 minutes

Seventeenth Place:

Barbara Ivy crewed by Linda Griesel and Rachel Smith (UK)

Finished Saturday 16th February 23:12 GMT – crossing time 76 days, 11 hours and 12 minutes

Eighteenth Place:

Dream Maker crewed by Elin Haf Davies and Herdip Sidhu (UK)

Finished Sunday 17th February 19:37 GMT – crossing time 77 days, 7 hours and 37 minutes

Atlantic Crossings Unplaced:

Mission Atlantic crewed by Andy Ehrhart, Mark Hefford, Nick Young and Justin Ellis (UK)

Finished Tuesday 5th February 12:28 GMT – crossing time 65 days and 28 minutes (re-supplied with food during crossing)

Atlantic Jack crewed by Cath Allaway and Margaret Bowling (UK)

Finished Wednesday 13th February 17:14 GMT – crossing time 73 days, 5 hours and 14 minutes (re-supplied with rudder pin and food during crossing)

Not mentioned here are "Titanic Challenge" who suffered a dramatic man overboard incident early on. Andrew Lothian was washed overboard, he was wearing a life jacket, but wasn't tied to the boat. Andrew spent 40 minutes in the water and was miraculously rescued by Jim Hook, his rowing partner in his own vessel. Miraculous, as this all happened in the dark in a rough sea! A mayday was called and the support yacht attended. Both men are safe, but made the difficult decision to retire from the race.

Again not mentioned is "Moveahead 2" who also encountered some problems, but nothing quite as dramatic as "Titanic Challenge" All four crew members are safe and well and were escorted by support yacht "Kilcudden" to be reunited with their families on the Cape Verde Islands. This must be particularly distressing, given two of the four crew members were on a second attempt, after the extraordinary story of their capsize and "double" rescue in 2005, described in "strange but true" earlier in the book.

Pairs Class Results - Atlantic Rowing Race 2007

First Place:

Gquma Challenger crewed by Bill Godfrey and Peter Van Kets (South Africa)

Finished Tuesday 22nd January 00:15 GMT – crossing time 50 days, 12 hours and 15 minutes

Second Place:

No Fear crewed by Nick Histon and Jon Csehi (UK)

Finished Tuesday 22nd January 06:05 GMT – crossing time 50 days, 18 hours and 5 minutes

Third Place:

Go Commando crewed by Orlando Rogers and Ben Gaffney (UK)

Finished Saturday 26th January 20:39 – crossing time 55 days, 8 hours and 39 minutes

Fourth Place:

The Reason Why crewed by Steve Gardner and Paul Harris (UK)

Finished Sunday 27th January 00:03 GMT – crossing time 55 days, 12 hours and 3 minutes

Fifth Place:

Pendovey Swift crewed by Ian Andrews and Joss Elliot (UK)

Finished Sunday 3rd February 08:46 GMT – crossing time 62 days, 20 hours and 56 minutes

Sixth Place:

Komale crewed by James Burge and Niall McCann (UK)

*Finished Tuesday 5th February 14:05 GMT – crossing time 63 days, 2 hours and 5 minutes
(please note due to extenuating circumstances this team started 48 hours after the main racing
fleet)*

Seventh Place:

Jaydubyoo crewed by Andrew and Joe Jordon-White (UK)

Finished Thursday 7th February 07:43 GMT – crossing time 66 days, 19 hours and 43 minutes

Eighth Place:

Row of Life crewed by Angela Madsen and Franck Festor (USA, France)

Finished Thursday 7th February 11:24 GMT – crossing time 66 days, 23 hours and 24 minutes

Ninth Place:

Ocean Summit crewed by Scott McNaughton and Neil Hunter (UK)

Finished Thursday 7th February 22:10 GMT – crossing time 67 days, 10 hours and 10 minutes

Tenth Place:

Pygram crewed by Fabien Decourt and Benoit Dusser (France)

Finished Wednesday 13th February 15:03 GMT – crossing time 73 days, 3 hours and 3 minutes

Eleventh Place:

Barbara Ivy crewed by Linda Griesel and Rachel Smith (UK)
Finished Saturday 16th February 23:12 GMT – crossing time 76 days, 11 hours and 12 minutes

Twelfth Place:

Dream Maker crewed by Elin Haf Davies and Herdip Sidhu (UK)

Finished Sunday 17th February 19:37 GMT – crossing time 77 days, 7 hours and 37 minutes

Thirteenth Place:

C2 crewed by Ian McGlade and Andy Watson (Northern Ireland, UK)

Finished Wednesday 13th February 22:45 GMT – crossing time 73 days, 10 hours and 45 minutes (please note C2 lost two race placements due to using more than 110 litres of their total ballast water)

Thanks to Woodvale for permission to reproduce all the official positions.

Thanks to Woodvale for allowing me to reproduce the following...

Steve Gardner, Paul Harris
"The Reason Why"

**Distance from San Sebastian de la Gomera, Canary Islands, Spain
to English Harbour, Antigua as the crow flies is
2931 miles (4727 km) (2552 nautical miles)**

Day	Date	Time	Latitude	Longitude	Progress		
		GMT	decimal	decimal	miles	km	n/miles
-1	Nov 30th 2007	2007-11-30 23:02:41	28.088 28° 5' 18"	-17.108 17° 6' 30"	2936 (-5 miles to day)	4725	2551
0	Dec 1st 2007	2007-12-01 23:06:51	28.088 28° 5' 18"	-17.108 17° 6' 30"	2936 (0 miles to day)	4725	2551
1	Dec 2nd 2007	2007-12-02 23:02:21	27.671 27° 40' 16"	-17.423 17° 25' 24"	2914 (22 miles to day)	4690	2532
2	Dec 3rd 2007	2007-12-03 23:03:01	27.269 27° 16' 8"	-18.129 18° 7' 43"	2868 (46 miles to day)	4616	2493
3	Dec 5th 2007	2007-12-04 23:02:51	26.902 26° 54' 8"	-18.867 18° 52' 3"	2821 (47 miles to day)	4540	2451
4	Dec 6th 2007	2007-12-05 23:04:11	26.411 26° 24' 39"	-19.643 19° 38' 34"	2770 (51 miles to day)	4458	2407
5	Dec 6th 2007	2007-12-06 23:05:51	25.895 25° 53' 42"	-20.516 20° 30' 57"	2713 (57 miles to day)	4366	2358
6	Dec 7th 2007	2007-12-07 23:02:51	25.609 25° 36' 34"	-21.293 21° 17' 35"	2663 (50 miles to day)	4286	2314
7	Dec 8th 2007	2007-12-08 23:02:51	25.258 25° 15' 29"	-22.411 22° 24' 39"	2592 (71 miles to day)	4171	2252
8	Dec 9th 2007	2007-12-09 23:01:41	24.871 24° 52' 17"	-23.445 23° 26' 42"	2525 (67 miles to day)	4063	2194

9	Dec 10th 2007	2007-12-10 23:04:01	24.505 24° 30' 19"	-24.246 24° 14' 45"	2473 (52 miles to day)	3979	2149
10	Dec 11th 2007	2007-12-11 23:04:51	24.076 24° 4' 34"	-25.155 25° 9' 19"	2413 (60 miles to day)	3883	2097
11	Dec 12th 2007	2007-12-12 23:02:21	23.574 23° 34' 26"	-25.913 25° 54' 47"	2362 (51 miles to day)	3802	2053
12	Dec 13th 2007	2007-12-13 23:02:31	23.109 23° 6' 34"	-26.652 26° 39' 7"	2313 (49 miles to day)	3723	2010
13	Dec 14th 2007	2007-12-14 23:01:21	22.607 22° 36' 25"	-27.474 27° 28' 25"	2259 (54 miles to day)	3635	1963
14	Dec 15th 2007	2007-12-15 23:04:41	22.060 22° 3' 37"	-28.251 28° 15' 2"	2207 (52 miles to day)	3551	1918
15	Dec 16th 2007	2007-12-16 23:02:21	21.484 21° 29' 4"	-28.940 28° 56' 25"	2161 (46 miles to day)	3477	1877
16	Dec 17th 2007	2007-12-17 23:02:51	20.957 20° 57' 25"	-29.575 29° 34' 29"	2118 (43 miles to day)	3409	1841
17	Dec 18th 2007	2007-12-18 23:03:01	20.360 20° 21' 35"	-30.013 30° 0' 45"	2089 (29 miles to day)	3362	1815
18	Dec 19th 2007	2007-12-19 23:03:41	19.600 19° 35' 59"	-30.508 30° 30' 28"	2056 (33 miles to day)	3309	1787
19	Dec 20th 2007	2007-12-20 22:04:41	19.011 19° 0' 39"	-31.318 31° 19' 4"	2004 (52 miles to day)	3225	1741
20	Dec 21st 2007	2007-12-21 22:04:01	18.544 18° 32' 38"	-32.164 32° 9' 49"	1949 (55 miles to day)	3136	1694
21	Dec 22nd 2007	2007-12-22 23:07:01	18.167 18° 10' 3"	-33.071 33° 4' 14"	1890 (59 miles to day)	3042	1643
22	Dec 23rd 2007	2007-12-23 20:05:41	17.998 17° 59' 52"	-33.863 33° 51' 47"	1839 (51 miles to day)	2959	1598

23	Dec 24th 2007	2007-12-24 23:06:11	17.854 17° 51' 15"	-34.885 34° 53' 5"	1772 (67 miles to day)	2851	1540
24	Dec 25th 2007	2007-12-25 13:07:51	17.743 17° 44' 36"	-35.329 35° 19' 44"	1743 (29 miles to day)	2805	1514
25	Dec 26th 2007	2007-12-26 23:05:01	17.585 17° 35' 6"	-36.485 36° 29' 6"	1667 (76 miles to day)	2683	1449
27	Dec 28th 2007	2007-12-27 23:01:53	17.540 17° 32' 24"	-37.225 37° 13' 31"	1618 (49 miles to day)	2605	1406
27	Dec 28th 2007	2007-12-28 23:04:13	17.501 17° 30' 4"	-37.830 37° 49' 49"	1579 (39 miles to day)	2541	1372
28	Dec 29th 2007	2007-12-29 22:05:03	17.412 17° 24' 44"	-38.497 38° 29' 48"	1535 (44 miles to day)	2470	1334
29	Dec 30th 2007	2007-12-30 23:02:53	17.125 17° 7' 31"	-39.212 39° 12' 43"	1489 (46 miles to day)	2396	1294
30	Dec 31st 2007	2007-12-31 23:02:03	16.949 16° 56' 55"	-39.932 39° 55' 55"	1442 (47 miles to day)	2320	1253
31	Jan 1st 2008	2008-01-01 23:01:53	16.959 16° 57' 34"	-40.741 40° 44' 27"	1388 (54 miles to day)	2234	1206
32	Jan 2nd 2008	2008-01-02 23:04:53	16.930 16° 55' 49"	-41.753 41° 45' 11"	1322 (66 miles to day)	2127	1148
33	Jan 3rd 2008	2008-01-03 23:02:43	16.950 16° 56' 59"	-42.547 42° 32' 49"	1269 (53 miles to day)	2042	1103
34	Jan 4th 2008	2008-01-04 23:04:13	16.968 16° 58' 6"	-43.322 43° 19' 20"	1218 (51 miles to day)	1960	1058
35	Jan 5th 2008	2008-01-05 23:03:53	16.956 16° 57' 21"	-44.090 44° 5' 23"	1167 (51 miles to day)	1878	1014
36	Jan 6th 2008	2008-01-06 23:04:43	16.953 16° 57' 9"	-44.903 44° 54' 9"	1113 (54 miles to day)	1792	967

37	Jan 7th 2008	2008-01-07 23:02:33	16.953 16° 57' 10"	-45.664 45° 39' 49"	1063 (50 miles to day)	1711	924
38	Jan 8th 2008	2008-01-08 22:02:03	16.952 16° 57' 8"	-46.571 46° 34' 16"	1003 (60 miles to day)	1614	872
39	Jan 9th 2008	2008-01-09 23:02:43	16.954 16° 57' 15"	-47.431 47° 25' 53"	946 (57 miles to day)	1523	822
40	Jan 10th 2008	2008-01-10 23:02:33	16.955 16° 57' 18"	-48.224 48° 13' 25"	894 (52 miles to day)	1438	777
41	Jan 11th 2008	2008-01-11 23:02:43	16.972 16° 58' 19"	-48.946 48° 56' 45"	846 (48 miles to day)	1361	735
42	Jan 12th 2008	2008-01-12 23:03:03	17.077 17° 4' 37"	-49.595 49° 35' 41"	803 (43 miles to day)	1292	698
43	Jan 13th 2008	2008-01-13 23:02:53	17.151 17° 9' 2"	-50.306 50° 18' 20"	756 (47 miles to day)	1216	657
44	Jan 14th 2008	2008-01-14 23:02:53	17.051 17° 3' 2"	-51.025 51° 1' 31"	708 (48 miles to day)	1140	616
45	Jan 15th 2008	2008-01-15 23:01:53	17.068 17° 4' 3"	-51.919 51° 55' 10"	649 (59 miles to day)	1045	564
46	Jan 16th 2008	2008-01-16 23:03:03	17.035 17° 2' 7"	-52.808 52° 48' 27"	591 (58 miles to day)	950	513
47	Jan 17th 2008	2008-01-17 23:02:53	17.076 17° 4' 34"	-53.540 53° 32' 25"	542 (49 miles to day)	872	471
48	Jan 18th 2008	2008-01-18 23:02:03	17.037 17° 2' 14"	-54.466 54° 27' 56"	481 (61 miles to day)	774	418
49	Jan 19th 2008	2008-01-19 22:03:03	16.978 16° 58' 39"	-55.261 55° 15' 38"	428 (53 miles to day)	689	372
50	Jan 20th 2008	2008-01-20 23:02:43	16.977 16° 58' 38"	-56.067 56° 4' 2"	375 (53 miles to day)	603	326

51	Jan 21st 2008	2008-01-21 23:03:03	16.958 16° 57' 28"	-56.918 56° 55' 4"	319 (56 miles to day)	513	277
52	Jan 22nd 2008	2008-01-22 23:02:23	17.016 17° 0' 57"	-57.967 57° 58' 1"	249 (70 miles to day)	401	217
53	Jan 23rd 2008	2008-01-23 22:02:03	16.995 16° 59' 43"	-58.981 58° 58' 53"	182 (67 miles to day)	293	158
54	Jan 24th 2008	2008-01-24 23:02:53	17.008 17° 0' 29"	-59.871 59° 52' 14"	123 (59 miles to day)	199	107
55	Jan 25th 2008	2008-01-25 23:02:13	17.013 17° 0' 48"	-60.745 60° 44' 41"	66 (57 miles to day)	106	57
56	Jan 26th 2008	2008-01-26 23:02:03	16.981 16° 58' 50"	-61.707 61° 42' 25"	2 (64 miles to day)	3	2
57	Jan 27th 2008	2008-01-27 16:02:03	17.007 17° 0' 27"	-61.765 61° 45' 53"	3 (-1 miles to day)	5	3

I suppose the last four and a half pages won't be that interesting to everyone, but I wanted to include the official daily positions and mileage as recorded by Woodvale.

The top ten tunes could be inserted here I think, that we listened to the most...

1. Woke up this morning – The Alabama 3 (single track, every morning!)
2. Golden Heart plus others – Mark Knopfler (album)
3. Foo Fighters – Echoes, Silence, Patience and Grace (album)
4. Green Day – Live, Bullet in a Bible (album)
5. Led Zeppelin – Various
6. The Verve – Urban Hymns (album)
7. Lynyrd Skynyrd – Freebird mainly, live track.
8. Muse – Origins of Symmetry (album)
9. Eagles – Hell Freezes Over (album)
10. Nirvana – Never Mind (album)

We also had audio books, Harry Potter, The Hobbit, The Hitch Hikers Guide to the Galaxy and Life The Universe and Everything. Sorry Paul, can't get your "Captain Beaky and his band" into the list !

The Morning after, Paul already minus his beard, we do a little P.R. for Zennor's "Mermaids Echo". Below, showing off my home made Antiguan flag!

English Harbour, with Fort Berkeley at its mouth on the right

View over English Harbour from Shirley Heights. Falmouth Harbour beyond

Stu and Andrea from "Sara", the "Oyster Shack" boys, Simon, Amanda, Joe, Andrew from P.A.Freight and us, at the Shirley Heights Sundowner over Montserrat

We met the minister for Tourism, the Hon. Harold Lovell, at a function they put on for us at Shirley Heights, and they fed us on traditional Antiguan goat stew! I was a bit dubious, but I have to say it was really tasty, and the rum punch was still good!

View from Breakfast at The Ocean Inn...looking down to Nelson's Dockyard

Galleon Beach, English Harbour   Left of centre in the trees, Ocean Inn

The Reason Why disguised as a dinghy!   The fort in daylight from Galleon Beach

You may have noticed that my beard has also gone, but it didn't go without a fight!

You've got to eat haven't you! Look closely at Mr. Obramovich's "boat" with yacht, "Sunseeker" and helicopter on board, just amazing, Falmouth Harbour, Antigua. Below-Joss and Ian arrived at 4.46am!! but we got up ... Monserrat still erupting

Just another tough day in Paradise!!

Random Memory No. 7

My head tells me there is nothing there, just endless miles of restless ocean beyond the black wall that appears at the edge of our world every night after dark. This black wall ends (or begins), where our navigation light has nothing to reflect off, past the ends of our oars.

Yet there it stands, without foundation or possibility, defying all thought, as sure, as solid and as resolute as any cliff of granite.

For the imagination is a very strange, but very strong thing, and even though I knew there was nothing there but ocean, over "the wall", as if to spite logic, stands a quay of stone.

And on this quay of stone, great wharfs of towering buildings loom, blacker than night, with great glassless windows yet blacker still. Silent sentinels lining the edge of a dark and brooding dockland world, inhabited by the unseen ghosts of a thousand lost souls, from a thousand half remembered dreams, waiting for the light so they can rest.

But I mustn't give the wrong impression here, for these are not scary places filled with terror, to be avoided at all costs, where the legions of the damned wait to devour any wayward vessel that should stray too close. These are places of welcome ... places of comfort and calm, though the ocean may boil around us. A haven and a hope in a sea of unrest, and an overriding reassurance for the mind that refuses to accept the extreme reality of the true situation.

I could never really see it as a solid form ... but I knew it was there ... in my mind's eye it was there, if not clear ... then certain ... not far off to port should I need to shelter. Or at least a thought of shelter , which it always gave without recourse, no matter how hard the wind blew, no matter how rough the sea became, no matter how black the night deepened ... awaiting The Grinning Turk, upon whose reappearance, this other world ... his moonlight trail, would cloak.

Have you ever thought you could see something out of the corner of your eye ... a light, a shadow, a star, a boat, only to find there was nothing there when you looked straight at it? With a little practice though, and keeping your eyes straight ahead, things are visible to the side, that are not when looked at directly ... a sort of lateral vision really. But with this lateral vision, there remains the question whether there is something there ... or not?

What I, or we are experiencing, although a little like that, is not the same, but purely something that is the product of the imagination, as there is no question that there is in fact nothing really there.

It is a strange feeling though, and the reason I say "we" is that having spoken to Paul about this, he told me that he too was experiencing the same feelings, thoughts and imaginings.

As early as the fourth night out, we were being pounded by waves when we deployed the sea anchor, but through all those uncomfortable, sleepless hours of uncertainty, noise and turmoil, my mind continually told me that we were merely in a channel between islands, and I could see it ... in my mind I could see it, and should the worst happen, and we needed to return to the haven of shore, it was but a little way to go, and well within reach. Even though it could never be seen with your eyes open, only with them closed.

This is still a clear memory to me now, and shows the power of the imagination when outside the usual comfort zones, as we were fully 200 miles out from the nearest land, which was The Canaries we had just left behind, and was actually in the wrong direction to where my mind's eye was showing me, but true distance and direction didn't matter, it was always there.

I always knew of course, there was no quay, no dock, no channel between the islands, and in fact no islands, but such is the power of the imagination, that it did comfort me still, and if not in full consciousness, it would spread a sub-conscious calm and reassurance through me.

Even when we were 1500 miles from anywhere ... further way from land than I ever dreamed possible, let alone likely that I would ever be, especially in a 23 foot plywood boat we built ourselves ... I ... we, don't ever remember being afraid.

Half Moon Bay, Antigua and "Smiling Harrys" bar complete with Cornish flag

Oliver, Samantha and Rebecca, The Galley Bar, complete with Rum and Tings!

A bit self indulgent, but I love this photograph, and I couldn't leave it out. And a post script as we come to the end of our time in Antigua, Alex proposed to Sam in the most romantic setting of Rendezvous Bay, Antigua, and they were married later in the year, in Zennor Church, back in Cornwall, before flying off for an adventure of their own in America.

I have to say that we had a fantastic time in Antigua, after we'd been through immigration that is. We had to go and queue up and fill in forms the day after we arrived, and the official was a real stickler, who read every word of every one, and then made everyone form a second queue at the other window, where after waiting for twenty minutes, the same bloke changed chairs and moved to the other window, and rubber stamped the forms he'd just checked earlier!!

We would have breakfast al fresco on the terrace looking straight over the pool and English Harbour, followed by a walk down to Nelson's Dockyard, where there are a few shops, hotels, bars and cafes. The road between Falmouth Harbour and English Harbour appears quiet in daylight, but is lined with bars and restaurants that burst into life after dark, and although we visited most of them, I can't remember having a bad meal. But then after the dried stuff Paul and I had been eating I suppose that was inevitable. We drank rum and "ting" in the "Galley Bar", and "The Mad Mongoose" on Falmouth Harbour, which was a favourite with everyone, as it seemed to have music most nights and didn't seem to close!

Restaurants in Nelsons Dockyard were pricey, but good, and "Catherine's Cafe" was a bit special, as it was on a pontoon, where the water came right alongside your table. This was the last meal we all had together, as Paul and family left the next day. It was also the night of Sam and Alex's engagement, and where we discovered Dauphinoise potatoes, but ever since, we have always called them Dolphin Noses!

I must tell you about Carl, from "Pura Vida", who went for a meal in a very expensive restaurant in Nelson's Dockyard, that had a tank full of fish, lobsters and shellfish, to choose your own. Carl picked a lobster, paid up front, and it wasn't cheap, and then completely dumbfounded the waiter, by having it set free in the harbour!! What a star.

We sat sipping pina colada in "The Admirals Inn" which seemed the epitome of colonial style, until the barman refused to make any more as he'd just washed all the shakers up ... again, and he wasn't going to dirty them anymore for us!! The Copper and Lumber Company was also dripping in colonial charm and atmosphere, and Amanda set her desk up in one of the internal palm clad courtyards, liaising with the boats still at sea, and selling A.B.S.A.R. t – shirts, (and sipping the odd rum I'd wager!).

During the day, the two beaches, Pigeon Beach on Falmouth Harbour, a ten minute walk away and Galleon Beach, in front of "The Inn at English Harbour" a 3 minute boat trip away, were beautiful white sand, and the sea was warmer than the shower at home. And both had great little beach bars that sold salads, open sandwiches, burgers and chips, and had bottles of cold Red Stripe or Wadadli, when it got too hot ... which was fairly frequent!

Traditionally, every Sunday evening, the "Shirley Heights Lookout", hosts the biggest party on Antigua, as the sun goes down. The view has got to be one of the most breathtaking in the World, even without the sunset, the rum punch is superb and the beer is cold. They have live bands and the place was jumping. The drummer's party trick, in one of the bands, was to have a bottle of Wadadli beer put in his mouth, where he held it, and proceeded to drink the whole bottle, one swig at a time, without using his hands, and without stopping drumming for a second! If all that wasn't enough, The Ocean Inn, our hotel, had a help yourself fridge on the terrace, and they left a notebook for you to write down each time you had a beer, and such trust, meant I marked down every one, and got into a lot of trouble when Chris went to settle up the bill!!

The only excursion we went on was to Half Moon Bay, which was worth seeing, and apparently you have to call in at "Smiling Harry's" 300 yards from the beach, so of course we did. You had to be a little careful of what you paid with, especially to the cab and mini bus drivers, as the currency is EC Dollars (East Caribbean), but most people like US Dollars and they are very different in value. You often thought you had a bargain, until they said no, US dollars, and it suddenly became expensive!

All too soon, our time in Antigua was over, and the only slight disappointment, was that only two boats arrived while we were there. We had looked forward to reuniting with all the friends we made in La Gomera, but it wasn't to be, and on our last night, there was only a handful of us left, along with Simon, Amanda, Stu and Andrea.

Paul and his family flew home on the 2nd February. Chris and our family were all booked on the 4th February, which ironically, is Sam's birthday. However, there was no room for me on the same flight, so I went back alone, by way of British Airways, a couple of hours later, with arrangements to meet up at Gatwick. It was odd being on my own in an airport in Antigua, it was odd there being no Paul, and having just been reunited with my family, it was very odd to be separated from them again.

As the sun sets on our time in Antigua, the adventure is nearly over.

Chapter 8 - "The Post Race Blog – The Final Chapter"

We had to leave "The Reason Why" again, which was hard. Not that we wanted to row anywhere, but it had been our home across The Atlantic, and to leave it moored up in English Harbour, waiting to be towed around to St. John's for shipping back to the UK, didn't seem right. Three days running it should have gone, but still it remained, until finally one day just before we left, it was gone! So we had to trust Simon, Amanda and Andrew of P.A.Freight to sort it all out and get the boat home, presumably on those same precision, purpose made and extremely expensive cradles!

So, the trip home for us was fairly uneventful, the flight I was on wasn't that full, and I had all three seats to stretch out in. This was not the case for Chris and the family, whose flight was packed to the gunnels, and wasn't that comfortable.

More farewells at Gatwick, as Sam and Alex left for Edinburgh, and the four of us remaining, started the first of two train trips home. Some 7 hours later, we were being picked up from Penzance Station, by my brother Alan, and then twenty minutes later, we were home.

It was very strange, as I had last been home on 20th November 2007, and it was now 5th February 2008, all the lead up to Christmas, the day itself and New Year hadn't happened, or at least it was as if they hadn't happened. Sipping rum with Paul, in a small boat, wearing "Santa's little elf" hats, in the middle of The Atlantic Ocean, 1500 miles from anywhere, didn't class as any sort of Christmas or New Year that I had ever known!

In a very magnanimous gesture, my first day back at work with Wombwell Homes, I found that John Wombwell, had not only booked a large table for lunch, for the whole office, but had The Globe, in Lostwithiel, decked out in Christmas decorations, and had a full Christmas menu arranged. Turkey, Christmas pud and all the trimmings, crackers, hats and balloons, all to make up for the Christmas Lunch I'd missed, it was special, and a big thank you once again goes to John.

The inevitable welcome home party, eventually happened on Saturday 16th February, but it got hijacked really as a final fundraiser to try and boost the money we had in the pot, while we were waiting for the return of "The Reason Why". The sale of which, would of course be the major amount we were going to donate to Cornwall Hospice Care, as we always hoped to aim for a total figure of around £25,000.00. So I sort of took it on myself to organise The Gurnards Head as the venue, and they rose once more to the occasion, as always, mixed a wonderful rum punch, which they called "Mo's Revenge" and donated the proceeds to the cause. We had an auction of Atlantic crossing related things, which Anthony Richards (Jen's Husband) did brilliantly. So brilliantly, that having somewhat reluctantly put "Droops" up for auction, in an effort to boost up the price a little, I only went and bought him back! Together with T-Shirts and Polo's, we raised a further £400, and all that was left to do, was sell "The Reason Why" when she arrives back in the UK in a couple of months.

Incidently, the £50 prize for the "guess how long we'll take" from before we left, was won by Ian Oliver from the Gig Club, with his guess of 55 days, 5 hours and 5 minutes, close!

Note: Because of the relatively short notice of this event, I have always felt a little guilty that not all of our fantastic sponsors could be there, and for that I am sorry.

4th April 2008

We have had news that "The Reason Why" is on her way back, and should arrive in a couple of weeks. There has been some interest in buying her so fingers crossed.

25th April 2008

"The Reason Why" returned to UK today, and Paul with son Jake, drove overnight and fetched her back. It was Rebecca's birthday, and we had a family "do" organised, so I think it very good of Jake to "volunteer" to go with his Dad, thanks Jake.

"The Reason Why" in one piece, in Newark, about to come back to Cornwall

The boat proved to be in pretty good order, which is more than can be said for the contents! The left over Pot Noodles, Go-Bars and dried food, is in the nearest bin! And as for the sweaty smelly clothes that were left in the cabin after the row, and have since been left to ferment in the Antiguan heat since the end of January followed by several weeks in a shipping container… they have followed the food!

What now for "The Reason Why?" There are a few people that are interested in her to take part in the Atlantic Rowing Race 2009. So she will be cleaned out and hopefully sold on to the next brave souls who decide to take on the challenge of living on "Mo" for weeks on end, beneath "The Grinning Turk", and perhaps with their own "Droops" and "Gus" for company.

25th May 2008

It looks like "The Reason Why" has new owners, and will be going off to sea again. Everything has been agreed subject to a marine survey, but neither of us see any problem and think she's ready to go again straight away!

We agreed to keep hold of the boat for a while, although the sale has been agreed with Jim Houlton and Paul Milnthorpe, who, as The Atlantic Vets, will be raising money for "Farm-Africa" and "Water Aid", and taking part in the Woodvale Atlantic Rowing Race 2009. Their website is, www.theatlanticvets.co.uk; and we wish them good luck and a safe passage, especially as they are keeping the name "The Reason Why", and they seem really nice guys.

28th June 2008

Woodvale prize giving day, at "The Tower" Hotel , Tower Bridge London, and on board "The Salient" for drinks, a buffet and a cruise on the Thames. I couldn't get Paul interested in going at all, no problem, he just didn't want to go, so Chris and I went, and I wouldn't have missed it for the world. It was great fun, meeting up with so many of the rowers we didn't see in Antigua, but there are a few other hazy memories, I won't elaborate on… walking across central London in a Dinner Jacket and flip-flops …a Transvestite bar … too much Stella … John Csehi and an enormous bottle of rum … Robbie Grant in a kilt … a slightly tipsy gig rower singing a version of "Trelawny" through the microphone at the presentation, and then proceeding to tell a stupid joke to a lady who had previously rowed the Atlantic, but who didn't laugh, she just walked away … you had to be there, but then it's probably better you weren't!

They presented me, with a goodie bag with a Woodvale cuddly toy and flag, a medal, a t-shirt with all our names on as we finished the race, a framed certificate and of course, the La Gomera Cup, which I think either Stu or Amanda brought back with them. I was going to take Paul's goodie bag but they said they would send it to him, probably just as well as things turned out, and we were driving from London straight up to Edinburgh the following morning, to see Sam and Alex.

The Woodvale presentation on board "The Salient", on the Thames, 28th June 2008

28th July 2008

A short video of "The Reason Why" leaving La Gomera at the start of the race has become available on line. Jen has brilliantly managed to put it in "The Final Chapter" on the website, and as I intend to keep the website pretty much forever, it should be available indefinitely. But the chap who took it and quite a few other videos of our start and other Atlantic Rowing Race starts, is Roger Haines, using "vimeo". You can see his website, and the "vimeo" website on line and see lots of the other competitors as well as us. We are "The Reason Why" #42.

Luckily, there is no video, short or otherwise, of my rendition of "Trelawny!"

Atlantic Rowing Race 2007

This is to Certify that

THE REASON WHY

Crewed by

Steve Gardner and Paul Harris

Has been Awarded

FOURTH PLACE

in the Pairs Class of the Atlantic Rowing Race 2007

La Gomera, Canary Islands to Antigua, Caribbean

with a Crossing Time of

55 days, 12 hours and 3 minutes

28th June 2008

Simon Chalk
for and on behalf of Woodvale Challenge Ltd

Dated

We arranged to meet Cornwall Hospice Care in Charlestown, their head office being St Austell, the CHC girls holding the oars, are Jane Appleton and Aimee Medlin.

So there we are, £24,000.00, the final total handed over in full to C.H.C

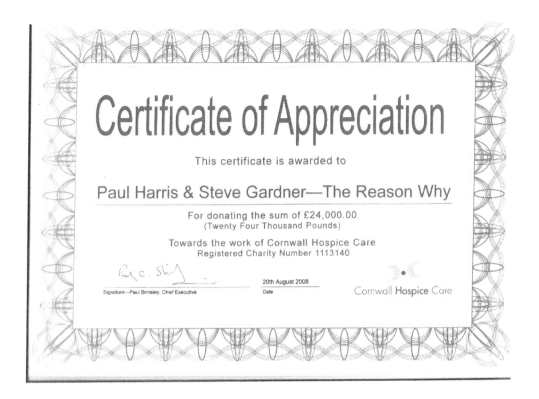

Certificate of Appreciation

This certificate is awarded to

Paul Harris & Steve Gardner—The Reason Why

For donating the sum of £24,000.00
(Twenty Four Thousand Pounds)

Towards the work of Cornwall Hospice Care
Registered Charity Number 1113140

Signature—Paul Brinsley, Chief Executive

20th August 2008
Date

Cornwall Hospice Care

August 2008

This was it, "The Reason Why" all hitched up and leaving Cornwall ....

.... Goodbye and fare well. It was a very strange feeling to see her go.

So there it is, the final moments, the money is all in and counted, including the money from the sale of the boat, and the photographs previously, show us handing over the most enormous cheque, in size and amount, so close to the target we set ourselves, that we cannot help but be pleased and proud.

And then two newspaper articles appeared, both photos and interviews were done, to both reporters, at the same time, at the cheque presentation to Cornwall Hospice Care, in Charlestown. Now do you think these papers have different readers?

Atlantic rowers hand over £24,000 to hospice charity

By PHIL GOODWIN
e-mail: pgoodwin@c-dm.co.uk
01736 365824
07966 622380

TWO Zennor Gig Club rowers who completed a gruelling charity race across the Atlantic have sold their boat and donated almost £24,000 to Cornwall Hospice Care.

Steve Gardner and Paul Harris completed the 2,956-mile Woodvale Atlantic Challenge in sixth place in January.

They took just over 54 days to row from the Canary Islands to English Harbour in Antigua.

Two rowers from Somerset have now bought their hand-crafted, state-of-the-art boat for £19,000 and plan to compete in the race in 2009.

The 23-foot vessel was christened *The Reason Why* after a line from Cornish anthem Trelawny, and should retain the name for the return trip, in line with nautical tradition.

Paul Harris, a technician for Western Power, said the pair were delighted to have raised so much money but planned to follow the advice of record-breaking Olympian rower Steve Redgrave, who famously asked to be shot if he ever got back in a boat.

"It was an unforgettable trip but it's so difficult to find the time away from work and fam-ily to do events like this," said the 49-year-old.

The duo followed in the footsteps of Olympic gold medallist James Cracknell and TV presenter Ben Fogle who competed in the Woodvale Atlantic challenge two years before, filming their progress for the BBC. In doing so they joined the ranks of an elite club of sportsmen - more people have climbed Mount Everest and been into space than have rowed across an ocean.

Steve Gardner, who at 51 was the oldest competitor in the race, recalled hair-raising moments coming within touching distance of tankers and ships.

"It was spectacular at times with pods of dolphins, whales and huge flying fish travelling through the air," said Steve.

Annie Binding, appeals manager for Cornwall Hospice Care, said: "It was an absolutely incredible feat and I take my hat off to the pair of them.

"It's not just the rowing but the amount of work they put in beforehand building the boat."

From left, Jane Appleton, Paul Harris, Steve Gardner and Aimee Medlin

---

Altlantic rowers say never again after 54 day battle with elements

Nude row racers big fund boost

by Sarah Glayzer
sarah@staustellvoice.co.uk

GETTING naked helped two Cornishmen row across the Atlantic and raise £24,000 for Cornwall Hospice Care.

Zennor gig club chairman Steve Gardner and club member Paul Harris raised the incredible total by completing the 2007 Woodvale Atlantic Rowing Race. Starting in La Gomera in the Canary Islands on December 2 last year, Steve and Paul crossed the Atlantic east to west, finishing in Antigua 2,500 nautical miles later on January 25.

Rowing au naturel was a tactic employed by Steve to cope with the hot and sweaty conditions aboard their boat The Reason Why; a name inspired by Cornish anthem Trelawny.

Steve, who lives in Zennor, said: "All inhibitions were quickly left behind. Rowing naked is not a gimmick because you get so hot and everything rubs and you get rashes and spots."

But, Paul, who is 42 and lives in Connor Downs, added: "My shorts were holding me together!"

Steve said the demands placed on his bottom by having to sit down for all 55 days of the race were "the biggest and most painful thing of the whole trip." To prevent their cheeks from chafing the men constructed a "bum hammock" to keep their sensitive behinds above the hard seat.

Judging by their finishing position the suspension of their buttocks certainly paid off, as The Reason Why finished sixth overall in the 22-boat race.

Unsophisticated toilet facilities were also part of the fun, with the men relying on a system they described as "bucket and chuck it".

"Whilst one of us was rowing the other was eating or sleeping so we didn't spend all our time together," said Steve.

Their achievement was made all the more impressive by the fact that the pair made their boat themselves.

Steve said: "The boat is a standard plan - it has to be because it's a race. We bought the kit and then made it ourselves. We sold the boat to help raise the £24,000."

Despite being one of 22 boats in the race, Steve and Paul were surprisingly isolated.

Steve said: "We were seasick for the first thirteen days as the motion on those little boats on the big ocean is different to anything else.

"After the first 24 hours we didn't see another boat. We were told we were within a mile of the Go Commando boat but we didn't see them."

The pair did however see plenty of tankers, the pilots of which didn't always see them.

Steve said: "The tankers were the worst, especially crossing shipping lines on the eastern side. Some of them didn't have their radios on so all we got was a beam bouncing back saying they were there."

Paul added: "There were ten tankers and a cruise ship we had to avoid. Some were as close as a few hundred yards away."

The friends, who have rowed together for nearly ten years, were on the mature side compared to some of the other teams competing in the race.

"I was the oldest bloke in the race," said 51-year-old Steve, "the team that beat us by just three hours - the royal commandoes - their combined age was 51!"

The demands of the race took its toll on the Cornishmen.

Steve said: "You can't physically eat enough calories for what you're burning off. I lost two and a half stone but I bulked up to sixteen and a half stone before I left.

"We were very thin and wobbly and it was difficult to stand up on shore as we had been on the boat for 54 days, and when we were on the boat we could stand up but we couldn't walk."

Paul said: "I don't see any point in rowing the Atlantic again; it's tempting fate."

After thanking their supporters, both men said they couldn't have completed the race without their onshore helper Jenny Richards who ran the website.

To learn more about Paul and Steve's race experiences visit www.the-reason-why.co.uk

CHARITY: Jane Appleton (left) and Aimee Medlin from Cornwall Hospice Care with Paul Harris (left) and Steve Gardner
Pic: Paul Williams

Without our sponsors, "The Reason Why" would not have participated in the 2007 Atlantic Rowing Race, so a big THANKYOU, from Paul and I, Jen and Droops.

Special thanks, for their constant support above and beyond the call, to:-

My wife Chris, Daughters Samantha and Rebecca, son Oliver and son-in-law Alex

Paul's wife Dawn, son Jake and daughter Danielle

My Mum, Hazel

Paul's Mum, Minnie

John and Maggie Wombwell and all at Wombwell Homes

Western Power Distribution

Alan Baumbach – for his advice, help, generosity, and the use of his boat shed.

A big Thank you to everyone else:- (and if I have missed anyone, sincere apologies)

Gwen Acott	Geoff Gilbert	Adrian and Teresa Montague
Ian and Sue Astrop	Richard Glasson	Andrew Montieth
Emma Beck	Malcolm Harding	Jacqueline Moore
Ren Beckerleg	Keith Harris	Mandi Moore
Lena Bennett	Terry Harris	James and Susie Morris Marsham
Simon Biggs	Nick Harvey	Mounts Bay Sailing Club
Jane Burn	Trilby Herriott	Leslie Osborne
Timothea Cardell	Andrew Hollingdale	Sylvia Pearson
The Cattran Family	Tom Hornsby	Scottie Penberthy
Mike and Viv Chadwick	Sally Ible	Chunky and Catherine Penhaul
Alice Clarke	Helen Jane	Simon and Adele Penrose
Richard Cornish	Jennifer Johnson	Mark Pilcher
Kay and David Curtis	Joy Kell	Annabel Pring
Roger Davis	Ron Kenyon	Kelvin Prisk
Chris Edwards	DW Leah	Helen Raine
Billy Faull	John Lees	Nigel and Kathryn Rescorla
Carl Ford	Paul and Jackie Louden	Dave Rhodes
John Forster	Serge Middleton-Dansk	Anne Roberts
Bill and Charmaine Francis	Gladys Malone	Alan Roberts
Sam Gardner	Cathy and Brian Milgate	Karen Ross
Pat and Penny Gibson	Wendy Mitchell	Bob and Nicky Robinson

Colin and Maria Rundle	The Globe Inn, Lostwithiel-
Adrian Rutter	& the 24 hr. Ladies Darts team
Sheila Saunders	Pemberley Developments
John Searle	Penwood Forge, B&B, Lostwithiel
Philip Shackleton	Projects Abroad
Shamrock Charitable Trust	The Property Shop, Lostwithiel and Bodmin
Michael Stapleton	Sailflags Penzance
Roger Stephens	Southlands Construction Services, Warwicks
Bill Stodden	St. Blazey Carpets
Karen Stone	Surfcornwall, Internet and Web Solutions
Brian Sullivan	Tim Acott, T.J.A. Surveying Services
Nikki Teague	Rob Whitney, T.O.G. (T.W.A.T.S.)
Nick and Pam Townsend	Truro Boat Owners
David Tresidder	The Wheelhouse, St. Mary's, I.O.S.
Andrew Turner	Lizard Trailers / Pump International Ltd
Barbara Wakefield	FAIRLINE (Menorca)
Cliff Warrell	The Gurnards Head Hotel, Eat Drink, Sleep
Roger Warren	The Tinners Arms
Roger and Kath Willett	Radius / Warren Grieg & Son
Gill Williamson	Cycle Logic
Brian Wills	Arco 2 / MTA Archtects
Roger Woolcock	Atlantic fm. radio/Pirate fm. radio
Jo Wright	John Nicholls Builders / H2OK
Nigel Young	Bennetts Fuels
A2 Rigging Ltd – Mel Sharpe	RS Developments / Nightsearcher
H Baumbach & Son, Hayle	This Is Cornwall / Mermaids Echo, Zennor
Bethells, Bideford	Horizon Utility Supplies / Clydesdale
BBC Radio Cornwall	Devington Homes
The Bucket of Blood, Phillack	Alan Leather Associates
Currie and Brown Widnell	Ward Williams Associates
Door Stop Ltd, St. Clement, Truro	Stephens & Scown / McMurdo
Farley Developments Ltd, Hants.	Ritelite / May Gurney
Flanagans Irish Bar, Pz.	And of course...
ER Jenkin and Sons, Pz.	Simon, Amanda and Tony at Woodvale.

7th Dec–Douglas Adams "Last Chance To See"

10th Dec – film "City Slickers"

12th Dec – Sir Winston Churchill

13th Dec - film "Topgun"

14th Dec – Albert Einstein

15th Dec – film "Good Morning Vietnam"

16th Dec – film "Zulu"

17th Dec – "Harry Potter" (a.t.o.o.t.p.)

18th Dec – Tommy Cooper

19th Dec – Woody Allen

20th Dec – Fawlty Towers

21st Dec – film "Breakfast at Tiffany's"

22nd Dec – film "Crocodile Dundee"

23rd Dec - film "Local Hero"

24th Dec – Martin Luther King jnr.

25th Dec – from "A Christmas Carol"

26th Dec – from "Allo Allo"

27th Dec – film "Back to the Future"

28th Dec – film "Flight of the Navigator"

29th Dec – Peter Pan

30th Dec – film "Gladiator"

31st Dec – Tolkien, "Fellowship of the Ring"

1st Jan – film "Star Wars"

2nd Jan – film "Pirates of the Caribbean"

3rd Jan – film "Monty Python and the Holy Grail

4th Jan – film "Falling Down"

5th Jan – film "Ghostbusters"

6th Jan – from Star Trek Next Gen

7th Jan – film "Braveheart"

8th Jan - film "Field of Dreams"

9th Jan – film "Dead Poets Society"

10th Jan – film "Rocky"

11th Jan – film "Shawshank Redemption"

12th Jan – film "The Shining"

13th Jan – film " Batman"

14th Jan – film "Blade Runner"

15th Jan – film "Jerry Maguire"

16th Jan – film "It's a Wonderful Life"

17th Jan – film "Dirty Harry"

18th Jan – film "Blues Brothers"

19th Jan – did not receive

20th Jan – film "12 Monkeys"

21st Jan – film "Jaws"

22nd Jan – film "Cool Runnings"

23rd Jan – Steven Redgrave

24th Jan – film "Casablanca"

25th Jan – film "Ice Cold in Alex"

26th Jan–Tolkien, "Return of the King"

Acknowledgements

To my Family, Chris, Samantha, Rebecca, Oliver and Alex for your total support as always, without which I could never have done this.

Paul Harris - rowing partner and friend...

A man of few words, but immense strength and resolve, (if no singing voice!)

A man of practical knowledge, skill, handicraft and seamanship without whom, "The Reason Why" would probably never have been built, our quest to row across The Atlantic Ocean may well never have been attempted, and this book, and the "blog" that inspired it may never have been written.

So he's got a lot to answer for!

(I did my share too, but I often had my Arthur Dent head on! – Steve Gardner)

"One day I may forgive him for super gluing my feet to that bloody boat!"

Droops

Jennie Richards ... the third member of "The Reason Why"

Jennie is the third very important member of "The Reason Why" being our daily (and nightly) contact for information, weather, positions and news from home. Jennie produced and ran the website, coordinated with sponsors, Woodvale and us. Jen translated "the blog," took out the 3 extra "J's", 2 extra "P's" and any unwanted "F's", "Mo" had added, and a big debt of gratitude is owed to Jen, for devoting her life before, during and after, to "The Reason Why", of which She is a part.

Steve Gardner

Acknowledgements – Photographic

Woodvale Challenge Ltd, for their kind permission to use the photographs, official positions, daily mileage records, the tracking beacon chart and the coloured dots of course, all from their website, and for being there. Thank you Simon and Amanda.

Chris Martin for the great shot of us at the start with Mount Teidy in the clouds

Jennie Richards and everyone who contributed to the Zennor Gig Club website

Ian Oliver for the Gurnards Head Barbeque and website photos

Nikki Robinson for the Scillies 2006 gig photos

Stu and Andrea on "Sara" for the mid Atlantic photos, for being good friends and for the gin!

Josef Lang for the River Danube photos

Paul Harris for all the photos on "The Reason Why" (my camera lead didn't fit the charger!)

Thank you all

Steve Gardner

Epilogue - So what happens now?

I have tried, but cannot fully explain the feeling of attempting and actually achieving a challenge so great as rowing The Atlantic Ocean. The sudden realisation that it is not "someone else", but *"you"*, attempting this thing. That it is *"you"* that other people are watching and not the other way around, and when they are gone *"you"* still have this thing to do. It is not *"you"* that walks away thinking, "I wish it was me" because *"it is you!"*

It is all encompassing, and fills your heart and mind all the time. It takes over your life in a way you never thought possible. Now it is over, and you remember very few of the bad times, only the good, and the pride of achievement and success. No real thought had been given to what happens after, or what do I do next? It reminds me of something someone once said after warfare, "we've won the war, now we must win the peace." And this can turn out far more difficult than you ever thought, in fact more difficult than the war!

Maybe you should work your way up the ladder of challenges, rather than leaping straight for the top rung, because trying to settle back into some form of normality is not proving particularly easy. I have been asked a thousand times "what's next?" Climbing Kilimanjaro? Cycling across America? What about rowing another Ocean?

Well, I decided I wanted to write this book, which has been sitting waiting to be finished and printed for three years, in which time Paul has organised, trained for, and achieved a cycle ride from John O'Groats to Lands End. When I see Paul and talk about the row, which isn't often, he says, "It is as if it never happened." I know what he means. But I can't just let it go.

I suppose finishing off this book and reliving every stage of the three years or so between 2005 and 2008, has brought it all back to life again, for me, and it fills all my thoughts again with an immense pride and passion, and not a little disbelief that one of the blokes in this book, who did this thing, is actually me!

So whatever happens now, there will be no "what if..."

I went rowing yesterday and thoroughly enjoyed it, and when I came home, I spoke to a mate on the phone who said that Claus Hein, (remember him at the start), wants to organise a walk across The Alps from his home town in Germany to Venice!

I wonder if he's taking elephants?

Steve Gardner

The Moonlight Trail

The sun dissolves in the western sky

Blue litmus soaked with liquid gold

Reflecting streaks

On shimmering peaks

As the daylight hours grow old.

As this ocean world once more turns dark

And waves unseen roll endless by

The flash of white

Phosphorescent light

Neath the black Atlantic sky.

The Grinning Turk rises up to spy

A million incandescent lights

Like a Holy Grail

Shines The Moonlight Trail

Through the everlasting nights.

We follow the silver path he paints

Until the first faint light of morn

When Polaris high

And Orion fly

In each bright new golden dawn.

Into The West goes The Reason Why

By the light of The Moonlight Trail

Cross the ocean wide

Like a ghost we glide

Without engine, fuel or sail.

As the Sun returns to reclaim her world

The Grinning Turk uneasy hides

Till the day so bright

Returns to night

And once more The Heavens rides.

sg2008

Lightning Source UK Ltd.
Milton Keynes UK
UKOW06n0908090714

234769UK00004B/18/P